Founded After Forty

How to start a business when you haven't got time to waste

by
Glenda Shawley

First published in Great Britain by Practical Inspiration Publishing, 2017
© Glenda Shawley, 2017
The moral rights of the author have been asserted

ISBN (print): 978-1-910056-46-2
ISBN (ebook): 978-1-910056-47-9

Practical Inspiration
PUBLISHING

Congratulations Kevi.

Best wishes for your future success.

Brenda x.

For my family, David, Pippa and Andrew... my forever *why*

Acknowledgements

Writing a book has been a long-held dream but without a push from my tribe, most notably Carole Ann Rice and the members of Fabulous Women and Marvellous Men, it would probably have remained just that, a dream. Thanks for giving me the push I needed.

Thank you to all the contributors in the book who gave of their time and experience so generously to take the book beyond the theory and into the real world. Thank you also to my 'test' readers whose feedback has helped shape the book for the better. I owe a debt of gratitude to all my clients over the last 24 years, without you I would not have a business or the motivation to keep on learning. Thank you.

Special thanks to my publisher and coach, Alison Jones, without whom this book would probably still be a work in progress. Thanks Alison for the insights, encouragement and gentle cajoling which have got me to the finish line. And thank you for the professional team that you have pulled together to turn my words into the finished book.

Finally thanks to my family. To Carol for the comprehensive and honest feedback that only sisters can give. To my niece Jenny and brother-in-law John for all their support. To husband David for the love, encouragement and compromises that have allowed me to run my business for the last 24 years and to write my book. To daughter Pippa who sets the writing bar very high. To son Andrew whose need to get on to his film set at 6.30 every morning got me out of bed at the crack of dawn to write this book. And last but by no means least to my wonderful parents for their ongoing love and belief in me, and Dad thanks for teaching me never to split an infinitive! Thank you.

Table of Contents

Introduction

If you are the reader I have in my mind's eye you are not a natural entrepreneur. If you were you would have several businesses, and probably a few failed attempts, under your belt by now. But whilst you are not a natural entrepreneur you do have a deep-seated desire to run your own business, to take control of your own income generation and to set your own retirement date.

You've probably raised a family to a stage of relative independence or maybe you've had enough of the corporate career. Maybe you can see the writing on the wall as your organisation is left behind by the technological revolution or perhaps someone younger starts shaking up the status quo and you recognise that it's time to move on. You may have realised that your retirement pension is not going to allow you the lifestyle you crave or perhaps the thought of a life without work scares you silly. Or maybe you've always wanted to see if you could run a business and it's now or never.

However, there's still a little voice inside your head asking, 'Can I do this? What do I need to do to make it work?' So this book is for you.

I've been there. In 1991 I was made redundant from my management career in Marks & Spencer. I'd always wanted to run my own business; redundancy was the push I needed. I've made many mistakes and learned a lot along the way. I'm still learning. Business isn't a constant. The marketplace is always changing, customer demands vary, new entrants change the competitive landscape, new technologies change the way we work. These are the challenges and opportunities that entrepreneurs thrive on. Are you up for the challenge?

How will this book help?

For years people in my network have been telling me I should write a book, but what book to write? Earlier this year I did some research and people said they wanted a how-to guide with examples from real people. People like them. Not multimillionaires, not gurus, but people they could relate to, people who were running small, locally based businesses on their own terms. They told me they didn't want another 'how to make six figures online whilst you sleep' type book. They wanted something that would lead them step by step through the process of starting and establishing a business locally. By locally I mean not online and not global. It might be hyper local... drawing customers from a radius of a couple of miles, or it might be a rather more flexible interpretation of what local means.

Whilst many of the steps in the book can apply to any business of any type, run by a person of any age, I have assumed that my reader is 40+, is based in the UK and wanting to run a business which is not primarily online. That doesn't mean that the business doesn't have an online presence, or that it doesn't sell via the internet at all, but it does mean that the internet is not where the main revenue comes from. As a more mature entrepreneur you have life experiences on which to draw but you don't want to waste time or energy making mistakes if you can help it.

I have tried to lead you gradually through the process of developing your business idea, planning for success, starting up and then the first few months of your business. In doing so I've used my own experience and some basic business principles illustrated with some real life examples from a varied selection of business owners. Most of the contributors acknowledge the mistakes they've made along the way and we've tried to share those in the optimistic hope they will help you to avoid making the same ones.

The book challenges you to think. But if you are like me you don't like to deface your book with notes so, whilst there are some examples of documentation you might use, the book is accompanied by a downloadable workbook, which is designed to become your business plan. That is a business plan for your own use. If you need a business plan to raise finance or to attract partners then it will give you the information for a more formal plan. Download your workbook, and find out how to obtain a printed version, at www.foundedafter40.co.uk.

I also realise the value of collaboration so we have a Facebook group: https://www.facebook.com/groups/Foundedafter40/ to accompany the book where you can pose your questions and support each other on your individual journeys. I'll be there too to encourage you on your way. If you need further help then it is available in online webinars... some free, some paid... and in workshops, a membership group, courses and away days. I know that for some of you the book will be all you need to fly but others would like more support, my aim is to offer you what you need. Please visit the website www.foundedafter40.co.uk to find out more.

Being realistic

Several themes were repeated in my interviews with the business owners featured in this book:

- Few had a robust plan when they started their business and those who did have adapted their plans as the business has developed
- Most didn't have a clear idea of their target market when they started and have refined their understanding of their ideal client by trial and error
- Business has taken longer to develop than expected
- Setting prices has been a challenge for most and is closely linked to self-confidence or the lack of it
- Running a business takes a lot of time and effort but can be a lot of fun
- Resilience is essential. You have to keep going when the going gets tough
- Support from family, friends and business associates is invaluable
- None of the business owners would want to go back to working for someone else!

I share these not to put you off but to help you to understand that things don't have to be perfect before you start. In fact if you wait for things to be perfect you will never start. The key is to get started and be willing to learn and adapt as you go. I hope that this book will be a constant source of reference as your business develops, that it will help get you off to a good start but will also help you to understand what changes might be needed and how to make them as time goes on.

I wish you luck but in the belief that we generate our own luck through consistent hard work and a willingness to learn and adapt. Above all I wish you success.

How to use this book

If you haven't yet started to work on your business idea...

If you are in the early stages of starting-up then I recommend you work your way through the book one chapter at a time. The book is designed to make you think and take action so it probably won't make good bedtime reading!

 This symbol indicates that there is an activity to do in your workbook, which can be downloaded from www. foundedafter40.co.uk. Each activity invites you to apply the information you are reading to your own business. You may choose to read the whole chapter and then go back to the activities or you may do them as you work your way through the book. However, I recommend that you at least start the activities contained in one chapter before you move on to the next as they are designed to develop your business idea incrementally. Some may take longer to complete, for example market research, so you may wish to put some action in place and then move on with your reading and come back to the activity when you have the answers. Some of the activities in later chapters refer back to those done earlier so will be much easier if you have done the work.

If you have already started work on your business...

If you've already made a start then there may be some chapters that are more relevant than others. The questions, summaries and action points at the end of each chapter should allow you to identify those where more work is needed. I suggest you take time to answer the questions and review your own actions and use that to decide whether or not you need to read that chapter but it would also be worth reviewing the relevant activities in the workbook to ensure that your business plan is fully thought through.

When your business is up and running...

I hope that you will continue to keep your business' development under review once your business is up and running and will refer back to the book to stimulate your thinking. The summaries at the end of each chapter should help you to identify which chapters to read again in more depth with the benefit of experience.

Getting extra help

I'm sure that I will not have answered all of your individual questions in these pages so do join the Facebook group https://www.facebook.com/groups/Foundedafter40/ for more support from me and other readers and check out the website, www.foundedafter40.co.uk, for further inspiration.

Every care has been taken with the information provided in this book and supporting material. However I am not a lawyer or an accountant and the law is complex and regulations change. Readers are advised to seek appropriate guidance to check current regulations as they apply to their particular circumstances before making personal commitments.

Part 1

Before you start

Chapter **1**

What's your 'why'?

'The more organizations and people who learn to start with WHY, the more people there will be who wake up being fulfilled by the work they do.'
—Simon Sinek, *Start with Why*

In 1992 I had a one-year-old baby, had taken voluntary redundancy from my management career and had a husband whose firm was shedding staff. I was also very conscious that my world revolved around my husband and daughter and that made me vulnerable; there would come a day when my daughter didn't need me and, if I wasn't careful, my husband might decide he didn't want a limpet clinging to him. I had two good reasons for starting my business. I had my 'why', but was it the right 'why'? Yes it made me start a business. Yes it made me push at my comfort zones. Yes it met my desire for independence and a life that didn't revolve around the needs of my husband and daughter. However, my 'why' led me to saying yes to everything that was legal, interesting and paid. I taught retail to English language students, life skills to young employees, CV writing to job seekers, and business administration to people who'd missed out on their formal education. I wrote training materials on mentoring and returning to work. I wrote newsletters, magazine articles and tender documents. I had as much work as I wanted but did I have a business? No, not really.

In his 2010 TEDx talk Simon Sinek suggests that those who lead the way in business and in life understand their *'why'*. I understood my *'why'* so why wasn't I leading in business? I had the wrong *'why'*! Sinek suggests that people buy 'why you do what you do' rather than 'how you do it' or even 'what you do'. So people buy from the therapist whose *'why'* is to eliminate pain in order that their clients can live a full life. They don't buy a sports massage because they want a sports massage per se, or necessarily because the masseur uses a particular technique. They buy because they share a desire to eliminate pain. The problem with my *'why'* was it was really self-centred, it inspired me, but wasn't a reason why people would want to do business with me. Why would anyone choose to buy so that I could be independent and provide for my family? They wouldn't!

If you are going to avoid my mistakes then you will want to find a *'why'* that inspires you *and* your potential customers. Your *'why'* will need to motivate you. It should keep you going when the going gets tough. And if you get your *'why'* right it can be the reason your ideal customer will do business with you rather than a competitor. Sinek suggests, 'the goal is to do business with people who believe what you believe'.

Giving back to help others succeed...

Fewer than 20% of cardiac arrest sufferers survive; **Jane Hardy** *was one of the lucky ones. At the time of her arrest Jane had a successful career in sales with a major finance company. That came to an abrupt end when she was made redundant following her recovery. It was time to re-examine her life and Jane felt that she had survived so that she could make a difference in the world; she describes it as 'giving back'.*

Initially this led Jane to retrain as a debt counsellor where she could put her wealth of financial knowledge to good use to help people to get out of despair. Whilst growing that business Jane came across networking; her first experience was not pleasant but she persevered and eventually she came across an organisation called Fabulous Women. She loved the ethos of collaboration and support and she soon became an Area Leader. When the founder decided that she could no longer keep the business going Jane stepped in because she didn't want it to go under.

Jane realised that she could develop the organisation to help owners of small businesses to succeed by connecting them with others who shared a similar goal. In less than three years the business has doubled in size, extended its reach beyond its Surrey heartland and has ambitious plans for growth.

Now renamed Fabulous Women and Marvellous Men the organisation allows Jane to live her 'why'. Her business is designed around the needs of its members and Jane is constantly looking for new ways to help. Not only is Jane 'giving back' by helping members to grow their businesses but also the domino effect as each of these businesses helps others means that Jane is able to impact on a much wider community.

Why is it important to understand your 'why'?

When you connect with the right 'why' for your business you will be able to make the decisions that will propel your business forward. If you know that you want to start a business but haven't yet decided what that business should be, connecting with the right 'why' might help you to find the big idea. You may be clear that your reason for being a massage therapist is to free people from pain so that they can live a full life and this means that you know what kind of people will want to use your services and their reasons for doing so. You will know what opportunities to say yes to and what to turn down.

My *'why'* wasn't serving me or my business. People were confused about what I did which made it hard for them to know what made a good referral for me. I was confused about what I did which is why I said yes to such a wide variety of projects. It's why I had work and not a business. Now my *'why'* is to help people to start and grow a small, locally based business so that they can enjoy success on their own terms. Now I make all my business decisions on how well they meet this purpose. My network has a much better understanding of what I do and, as a result I get a steady stream of interesting, relevant and profitable referrals.

Getting to your *'why'*

I suspect that you have a reason for wanting to start a business. Perhaps you've been made redundant and now want to control your own future. Perhaps the children have become independent and now you want to do something for yourself. Perhaps you want to supplement a retirement income. These are all laudable reasons for wanting to run a business but they will not give others a reason to buy from you, or you a basis for your decision making.

I hope that you also understand that you are in business to make a profit. The need for profit will underpin some of your decision making but unless money is one of your core drivers it is unlikely to inspire you for long and it won't inspire people to buy from you.

The chances are that you'll find your real *'why'* when you examine your core values. You might like to think of it as your mission. What have you always put first? Is there a cause or an idea that you feel passionate about? If your mother was describing you to a friend who'd never met you what would she say (I'm talking mother bragging rights here not a list of your misdemeanours!)? What qualities would your closest friends attribute to you? What did your last work appraisal say about your contribution? Your *'why'* may well be found in the answers to these questions.

On a mission...

Leonie Wright used to suffer from high blood pressure and frequent migraines and found herself on regular medication. All this changed when she changed her diet, her blood pressure is now normal and she no longer suffers migraines. Leonie is now on a mission to help other people live a healthier lifestyle through better food choices. Since training in nutrition in her native Holland she has been running Eat Wright helping people to get healthy, lose weight and feel better.

The more artist **Rosanna Henderson** explored mosaics, the more passionate she became about the medium as an art form. Rosanna realised that most people's experience of mosaics is limited to crafts and mass-produced bistro tables. She wants to change that by raising awareness of the fantastic artistic potential that mosaics have as well as their long history going back to the Romans. Rosanna is on a mission to get mosaics treated as a serious art form and displayed in art galleries, exhibitions and as community art projects.

Quite often other people see what we don't. This is where the Johari window technique can be helpful. If you haven't come across this before it is a psychological tool developed by Joseph Luft and Harry Ingham in 1955. The Johari window considers four areas of insight:

- What we know about ourselves that others also recognise in us
- What we know about ourselves that others can't see
- What others see in us that we don't recognise
- Those qualities that neither we nor those who know us are aware of

The window is often represented as a diagram:

	Known to self	Unknown to self
Known to others	Open self: information that we know about ourselves which is also understood by others	Blind self: information that others have about us but which we have not recognised
Unknown to others	Hidden self: information which we understand about ourselves but which is not recognised by others	Unknown self: those qualities that neither we nor those who know us can see

Many people find it really hard to connect with their *'why'* because they try to find it within themselves but as the Johari window demonstrates, that means we only have about half of the picture. Sometimes we overlook the obvious. There are some things that are so innate to who we are that we stopped seeing them years ago. However, they are things that may be very clear to your family, friends and colleagues. So if you are struggling to find your *'why'* start by asking for some help from those who care about you.

Getting to her 'why'...

*After 10 years in a high flying corporate career **Monica Castenetto** wanted a change that allowed her a more balanced life. She tried lots of things including garden design, photography, film-making and contemporary dance but still hadn't found her purpose in life. Surviving a brain tumour at the age of 42 made Monica realise that she wanted to use her talents to help other people, but how...?*

> *It was a chance conversation with an acquaintance that led Monica to life coaching. Her friend pointed out that Monica had a wealth of real life experiences and had worked in so many different fields that she would be superbly qualified to help others find their way through life's challenges. At the time Monica didn't know what a life coach was but when she researched it she realised that she had found her calling. Not only did being a life coach enable her to help others but it also allowed her to use many of the skills she had acquired over time and live the balanced life she craved. She had found a 'why' that would appeal to others whilst also meeting her own needs, now all she had to do was to turn it into a business!*

You have a *'why'* but do you have a business?

Of course it's possible that your *'why'* is driven by an existing passion but before you rush headlong into business, stop. Take off the rose-tinted spectacles. Ask yourself if you can really make a business out of your passion. Sadly people don't always value what you do or share your passions sufficiently to pay enough money for them.

Are your friends suggesting that you turn your hobby into a business? Do they keep asking you to make something for them? Do they pay you enough money to cover all the expenses, including your time and an element for overheads (e.g. marketing and administration) and to make a profit? If they do then you may well have the basis for a sound business. However, if your friends are not paying a realistic price you do not yet have the evidence that your hobby will become a good business. We'll talk about ways to establish the business potential in chapter 6.

Is your *'why'* based on an interest or a cause that you are passionate about? Fantastic, but does it have business potential? Will it generate a product or service that enough people will pay enough money for, often enough, for you to have a business? If you can't make your interest or cause the root of your business then you may need to have a more conventional business and commit to the cause in another way. For example TOMS shoes has a one for one programme where for every purchase a person in need benefits. Would adapting this idea help you to achieve your *'why'*?

What would success look like to you?

'How do I define success? Let me tell you, money's pretty nice. But having a lot of money does not automatically make you a successful person. What you want is money and meaning. You want your work to be meaningful, because meaning is what brings the real richness to your life.'

Oprah Winfrey

Success means different things to different people but when you are setting up in business the only definition that matters is yours. There are plenty who measure success in terms of money and the trappings that go with it but if your *'why'* is about making a change in the world you may measure success in terms of impact. If your *'why'* is to relieve pain and suffering you will measure success in clients who are now able to live life to the full where previously they were limited by their pain. One of my measures of success is the number of thriving businesses I have helped to create.

When you understand your *'why'* and your definition of success you will be well placed to design a business that meets these goals. You will be able to ask the right questions of yourself and others, then you will make the right decisions and spend your time working on the right things.

You may well measure success in a number of different ways and your ideas will probably change over time. You may therefore want to think of success in the short, medium and long term. Again how you define these is up to you. If you are 45 you may see long term as 30 years but at 70 even 10 years might feel too far into the future!

Here are some ideas you might wish to consider in designing your vision of success:

- Numbers of people you have helped
- Your clients' achievements
- Changes that you have influenced
- Your contribution to society
- Your work-life balance
- The money you have made
- The investments your business has enabled

Connecting to your vision of success

Defining your vision of success at the outset is really helpful but it's all too easy to forget that vision as you get sucked into the day to day challenges of running your business. It's therefore important to find a way of reminding yourself what you are trying to achieve. You may wish to try one or all of the following techniques:

Visioning

This is a technique where you imagine yourself enjoying the success you were planning for.

Suppose that your vision of success is to win a contract to supply your organic fruit juice to Waitrose. Close your eyes and picture yourself walking into a branch of Waitrose and seeing your fruit juice on the shelf. Make the vision really vivid. What can you see as you walk towards the fruit juice aisle? Perhaps you can see people queuing at the tills with your organic fruit juice in their trolleys. What can you smell? Perhaps you have to pass the coffee shop with its aromas of freshly brewing coffee or maybe the bakery is filling the air with the smells of fresh bread. What can you hear? Maybe you are empathising with a mother being pestered by her infant or perhaps you can hear a sales person encouraging people to try your organic

17

juices. See yourself picking up the small, clear plastic glass and tasting that smooth fruity juice you have spent so much time perfecting. You turn the corner... and there's your organic fruit juice filling a shelf at eye level, the labels you spent hours deciding upon facing out to entice the customer to pick up and buy. And that is just what you see several customers doing. How do you feel?

This is a powerful technique and can help you to work out some of the decisions that you'll need to make as you develop your business. In this example our fruit juice maker pictured her bottles on the shelf with their labels facing out. This image would get her thinking about the shape and colour of the bottles, the font, colour and illustrations used on the label. She will think about making her product stand out from the crowd whilst also connecting with the *'why'* she went into that business. So if her *'why'* is about providing healthy, low-sugar beverages that children will want to drink her labels should get that message across and appeal to children and parents.

 If you think that the visioning technique could work for you make sure that you are at the centre of the picture and try to connect with all of the senses: sight, sound, smell, taste and touch. The more senses you can imagine the more vivid and compelling the vision.

Vision board

This technique can work on its own or alongside the visioning. Your vision board will be a physical representation of what you are trying to achieve. You may build a collage of images and words to construct a picture of your vision of success. You then pin this picture up where you will see it often. Other people make their vision board in Pinterest where they can add images as they see them.

Vision boarding is highly visual and works best for those of us who favour the visual processing of information. If you use this technique make sure that you look at your board on a regular basis especially when you have decisions to make. Ask yourself, how will this decision take me towards my aim?

Some people simply set themselves a numerical goal e.g. number of new names added to a mailing list or a sales target and they post that large and very visible, for example on, or close to, their computer screen so that they are always focused on one thing.

Affirmations

Many of the success gurus recommend using affirmations as part of our daily practice. The principle is based on the need for a positive mindset so an affirmation should be a positive statement of what we want to believe. The idea is that if we read our affirmations aloud every day they will influence our mindset for the good. They will help us to overcome self-doubt and that unhelpful inner voice that questions our ability.

So an affirmation needs to be written in the first person and in the present tense, for example:

- I have all that it takes to run a successful business
- I choose to think positive thoughts
- I am good enough
- I believe in myself

To quote self-development expert Brian Tracy, 'Whatever you believe with feeling becomes your reality'. He recommends reading out our affirmations frequently throughout the day so that they become part of our belief system.

Reminders

Whether or not you find visioning, vision boarding or affirmations helpful you do need to find a way to stay connected with your *why* and your vision of success. You need to find a way that works for you, if you don't I guarantee that you will get so caught up in the day to day activities of running your business that you will lose sight of where you are heading. Here are some ideas for staying in touch with your *'why'* and your vision of success to consider:

- Use Post-it notes on your computer screen or in your diary to remind yourself of what you are trying to achieve
- Set a regular reminder on your phone or desktop
- Develop a mission statement to explain your *'why'* and display it on your office wall, on your website and share it on social media
- Join an accountability group, hire a coach or mentor or ask someone close to you to check on your progress regularly

Start with the end in mind

Your vision of success may have included an exit strategy for your business but if it didn't it's a good idea to think about this at this early stage. Do you want a business that will fund your retirement or provide an inheritance for your children? Do you want to pass on the business to your children as a going concern? Do you want a business that can continue to run but without as much of your active involvement as your circumstances change? Do you see yourself continuing to work until it's time to meet your maker? Or will you just close your business when you've had enough?

 Your answers to these questions will help you to determine what kind of business you want to run and how to set it up. For instance if you want a business that you can sell to fund your retirement or to provide a nest egg for your children then it will need to be able to function without you. There will need to be some value in the business that is independent of your skills and expertise.

However, funding your retirement from your business doesn't necessarily involve selling the business. Can you find something that will provide you with a residual income? Perhaps you can develop a product that will continue to sell with little fresh input from you. Could a new management team take over the day to day running of the business whilst you retain a sizeable shareholding? The desire for a residual income is one of the reasons why so many people go into network marketing so that they can continue to earn from the efforts of their team as they begin to work less. This is an option I discuss more fully in the next chapter.

In summary...

- Your *'why'*, or mission, might be the differentiating factor that will make people buy from you. That *'why'* will keep you going when things get tough
- Understanding your *'why'* will help you to clarify what your business is and enable you to make effective decisions
- Your *'why'* is likely to be closely aligned to your core values
- People who know you well may help you to connect with things that you don't see for yourself
- Developing a vision for success and finding a way to stay connected to it will help to keep you on track
- Being clear about your end goal will help you to shape your business to achieve that goal in the timeframe you set

To get you thinking...

- What is my purpose in life? What's the legacy I want to leave?
- How does this purpose turn into a business?
- Where do I want to be in 5, 10, 20 years' time? What role does my business play in this vision?

Action points...

- Explore your *'why'* to find one that makes you happy and attracts customers
- Turn your *'why'* into a mission statement that you can display where you will see it often and use it to attract your ideal client
- Write down your vision for success
- Find at least one technique to stay in touch with your vision for success

Chapter **2**

Choosing a business model that is right for you

'If you do what you love, you'll never work a day in your life.'

—Unknown

Now I'm not implying that running a business will not involve hard work but if you can find a business based on something you love it will be work you are happy to do and may feel more like fun. So what kind of business are you drawn to?

Perhaps your *'why'* and your vision of success make the choice obvious. Maybe you have a skill, a passion or some experience that will be the basis for your business. In this case you'll probably start your business from scratch but if you don't have a clear business idea you'll need to look for other options.

Franchising

To an extent your options will depend upon your attitude to risk. If you want a relatively safe option then consider franchising. Franchising allows you to buy in to a proven business model, which reduces the risk and makes the business a more attractive proposition for the banks if you need to raise funding. Franchise opportunities come in all shapes and sizes with the investment required ranging from just a few thousand to several hundred thousand pounds. As a franchisee you will be expected to follow the business model established by the franchisor and will have limited room for your own creativity. However, the business is yours and, although you will pay continuing fees to the franchisor, it can be a great way to make money and learn how to run a business.

If you are considering franchising there are a number of franchise shows each year that give you an opportunity to consider your options all under one roof. If you are thinking about franchising there are a number of things you should do before reaching a final decision:

- Research the organisation thoroughly and do your due diligence to ensure that the organisation is on a sound financial footing, bona fide and that there are no nasty surprises in the terms you have to sign up to
- Talk to existing franchisees about their experience e.g. how happy are they with the support they get from the franchisor; is the information about costs and profit potential accurate; what are the advantages and disadvantages, positives and negatives of working with the company?
- Read and thoroughly digest all the information supplied by the franchisor. What support can you expect? What are the continuing costs? How much flexibility will you have to make your own decisions?
- Be really clear about all the costs involved. What does the fee payable to the franchisor cover? How much more money will you need to invest to get the business off the ground? For example, a franchise fee will probably not

include premises so how much will it cost you to rent suitable ones and what other costs will you also need to pay?

These are just some of the things that you will need to consider before you decide to go for the franchise model. For more information look out for seminars on the topic and visit The British Franchise Association for lots of objective guidance and a list of accredited franchise operators (www.thebfa.org).

A personal story from a franchisee...

Cathie O'Dea has always loved to travel however after more than 30 years working for some of the big names in travel she was becoming disillusioned. A friend suggested she look at Travel Counsellors, a franchising company based in the north of England. She liked what she saw and was accepted after a short interview and with the testimonial from her colleague. (Travel Counsellors do expect their new franchisees to have at least four years' experience in the travel industry and there are other terms set out in the franchise document.) Cathie is still happy with her decision 10 years on and wishes she'd taken the leap earlier.

What are the advantages?

- *Freedom to run her business in a way that suits her with the backup of a large company for support*
- *Professional marketing and administration*
- *24-hour help desk so Cathie knows that her clients can always get help even if she isn't available whilst they're away*
- *In the very rare event of a complaint the team at head office is available to help*
- *A team of over 850 fellow Counsellors whom she can consult for specialist expertise when a client has an unusual request*

- *Cathie can usually arrange for a colleague to cover her holidays, unusual for a business owner*

Of course this support comes at a cost. As well as a monthly administration and insurance fee that Cathie has to pay, Travel Counsellors take 40% of every sale. Cathie feels it's worth this for the guarantees that being a part of a big organisation give her.

Things to be aware of:

- *It takes time to build a client base especially if you can't take your contacts from your previous job*
- *Income is unpredictable and payments may be made several months after the work is done especially in the travel industry when customers may book months in advance but only pay the full invoice a few weeks before travel*
- *Working from home can impact on family life. Work can spread to take over the house and it can be difficult to switch off which can lead to some tension in the family*

Whilst most of the marketing is done by head office Cathie does network extensively and makes a point of asking her happy clients for testimonials and referrals. She has her own page on the Travel Counsellors website where there is a search facility for people to find a local agent. Cathie also makes good use of social media to demonstrate her love of travel and expertise in the industry.

Here are Cathie's top tips for someone taking on a franchise business:

- *Don't expect instant success, it can take up to two years to see real progress*
- *Believe in yourself*
- *Chase the business; it won't come looking for you*

> *Gilles and Claire Pelenc own two businesses, one a franchise and the other in network marketing.*
>
> *Their franchise business, Athena, was a well-established business-networking organisation with potential for growth. Gilles says 'The advantage of starting a franchise is that you walk into a profitable business straight away. Within six months we had made our initial investment back and were in profit, with a business model and a system that were very easy to implement, with support and training from the franchisor. Although we put in a lot of work to generate growth, the tracks were laid for us, all we had to do is go to work and dictate our own speed...'*
>
> *Gilles and Claire now have a business that they will be able to sell on when the time is right.*

Network marketing

Network marketing is another good option for the risk averse and offers a very flexible business opportunity, which can make it a really good option when you have other commitments or are semi-retired. Network marketing is also referred to as multilevel marketing. There are two ways to build your network marketing business: firstly by selling products and secondly by recruiting more people to your team which allows you to earn a percentage from their sales too. Some of the big names in network marketing include: Forever Living, Arbonne, Utility Warehouse, Stella & Dot and more.

The initial investment in a network marketing business is often very low and, providing you are in the right team with the right company, there is a lot of support from your team leader and the organisation. However, if you already know a lot of people in the area who are with the company you are considering you may find it difficult to break into the market. Can you reach out beyond your local area for customers and team members? Are the local networking groups saturated with owners from the same network marketing company and if so, how will you build your business?

As with franchising you will need to follow the guiding principles of the company you are with but there is some scope to design your business to suit your lifestyle. Top earners can build a business that allows them to live comfortably and to leave their business to their loved ones in their will, but if you just want to make a little extra money to top up your pension that's perfectly possible too.

If you are considering a network marketing business here are some things you'll need to think about:

- Do you like the products of the company you are considering joining?
- Do you enjoy talking to people and selling products?
- Do you have a wide network of contacts who might be interested in the products or the business opportunity and, if not, are you prepared to work to build one?
- Do you like to work in a team?

A personal story from a network marketer...

Jill Bennett came to network marketing when her high-flying civil service career was no longer serving her needs. She wanted something that allowed her some flexibility around her family life and that is what Arbonne International offered her.

Amongst the advantages of network marketing are:

- *Low start-up costs*
- *There is a system for success so you can follow the model without any need to reinvent the wheel*
- *All the products are developed for you*
- *The legal aspects are taken care of*
- *You get a website free and it's looked after for you*

- You can leverage your time to earn money on many occasions for work done just once
- You can bequeath your business with many companies once you reach a certain level

Jill has a few tips for those people considering going into network marketing:

- You must love the products/services you decide to work with and use them so that you can talk with passion and be authentic when sharing them with others.
- You must like/love your sponsor and feel you can work with them.
- You must be prepared to be coachable and willing to accept help, especially if you haven't worked this sort of business before.
- You must be prepared to work – it is netWORK marketing after all. You can work your business full time, part time but not sometimes; you need a level of commitment and consistency

And Jill's tips for finding the right opportunity:

- Look for a company that is at least five years old and is a member of the DSA (Direct Selling Association – the regulatory body for the profession)
- Make sure the company you're joining has a good multimedia training strategy in place

But as Jill says it isn't all plain sailing, you need to have self-motivation and a strong 'why' to keep you going. There is a very high dropout rate because people leave the business – it's easy to get in and easy to drop out! Whilst it's a very simple business it's not always easy. You need tenacity and strength to keep on going when you get disappointments, such as people leaving your team.

Rethinking network marketing...

Giles Button *had owned his business for 17 years and had offices and a team of 20 people but he was looking for a new challenge. What he wanted was a flexible business that he could work around his lifestyle where he could leverage his time and not simply swap time for money.*

Although initially he'd dismissed network marketing as a 'bit of a scam or pyramid scheme' when he discovered that Harvard Business School was teaching it as a business model he decided it was time for another look. He realised that the industry had come of age and could provide him with the type of business he was looking for. There would be some financial investment but he wouldn't need employees or expensive business premises and he could work the business around his other commitments.

Giles started his network marketing business in exactly the same way as he would start any new company and drew on all the business experience he had acquired over the years. He created a 12-month and 5-year plan, with SMART targets and also a realistic financial projection. Giles believes that too many people go into network marketing expecting an instant return, which just isn't realistic in any business. As with all businesses it takes time to get established.

Gilles Pelenc on choosing your network marketing company...

Gilles recommends doing your homework and choosing well. He says there are a lot of great companies with good track records but others who patch over the cracks 'throwing glitter in the eyes of the greedy newcomer'.

> Whilst a brand new ground floor opportunity might have great potential there will be little training or support so you will have to find your own way with a company that may not be there in two years. However, the disadvantage of an established company is that there will be a lot of people already involved even though the average person on the high street may never have heard of the company. On the plus side, a company that has been trading successfully for a number of years has the systems, support and training in place to help you succeed in your business.

Buying an existing business

Another lower risk alternative is to buy an existing business. Again it will be really important to do your due diligence to ensure that the deal you are being offered is genuine and based on accurate information. You will need an accountant to help you validate the financial information and a lawyer to check the legal agreements. You will also need to check that there are no charges against the business, no covenants that could come back and bite you after you've sold the business (for example if the person you sold to defaulted on an obligation) and that the business owns everything you are being asked to pay for including intellectual property (for example patents, trademarks, designs and copyrights).

The advantage of buying an existing business is that you are buying a going concern so there should be some value in an existing customer base. Make sure that any customer information is included in the deal. You should also look for opportunities to add value to the business. Could you extend trading hours or add another service or product line? Is there untapped capacity that some more marketing could fill? If you can't find a way to increase turnover and profits you may be paying maximum price for a business that has reached its full potential and you need to be careful that the business isn't on a downward trajectory. This is where your professional advisers can help but also take a good look at the business yourself. Ask the owners lots of questions:

- Why are they selling?
- What are the trends in the business?
- What changes have they made to the business over time?
- What marketing do they do?
- Where do most of their sales come from?

If it's a bricks and mortar business visit at different times of day and on different days of the week to build a fuller picture of the actual trading position. Is what you see consistent with the financial and trading information you have been given? Talk to other local business owners about the area and the business, you may be surprised about how much they know! Talk to some of the customers if you can, but be discreet, as the fact the business is for sale may not be public knowledge and uncertainty about the future can undermine a business.

Do an online search. Are people talking about the business and if so what are they saying? If there are any local Facebook groups you may well find some comments there. Join the group and ask for recommendations for the type of business you are considering buying; see what people say about your target.

Ask yourself lots of questions too:

- What changes would you want to make to the business and would those appeal to the current customers? If not you could be paying for goodwill that will have no value to you (but is valuable to the vendor)
- How much will you have to spend on any changes you might want to make to the business/premises etc.?
- Can you see opportunities to grow the business by doing more marketing or adding to the current offer? Is the owner making full use of the online potential for the business?
- What changes are happening in the area and will these affect the business? Think about residential and commercial property developments; changes in infrastructure e.g. road building; changes in the local population etc.

Jane Hardy on buying a business...

Jane bought a business that she had been a part of but that didn't mean she knew it all. She shares some of the lessons she learned:

'Make sure that you do your due diligence in great detail. Don't assume that everything you're told is accurate. Examine the financial information with a fine toothcomb. Take professional advice but make sure that your experts have the right qualifications and experience to help you and will spot issues and ask questions you might not think of. Talk to existing customers and staff to get a feel for the accuracy of the information and an understanding of what's working and where there is scope for improvement.'

Key Lessons learned:

- *Bring in expert help from people who share your vision as soon as possible*
- *Bring a coach on board from the start to give you a sounding board and an outside perspective*
- *Don't wait to make key changes that will impose your ideas on the business*
- *Be prepared to take difficult decisions to establish who is boss*
- *Expect the unexpected and be prepared to adapt your plans to take account of new circumstances*

Spotting untapped potential...

Roy Summers *bought the personal training studio that he worked in because he could see opportunities that the then owner wasn't tapping into. At the time he didn't have much of a plan just a commitment to keep working hard and to fix the things* *that were broken to give the studio a more professional image. Roy knew that he could improve the business' reputation and that there was plenty of scope for growth with more marketing and an additional trainer.*

Roy admits that it has taken five or six years and input from a number of other business people, including his accountant, to develop a clear business plan. However, he now has a clear vision and an exit plan. The business has been growing consistently year on year for the last five years and Roy is continuing to invest in the business and bring in new services to grow it still further.

Starting from scratch

This may be your best option if you are following a passion or a dream. However, it is probably the most risky option because you really don't know whether your idea is commercially viable. You will need to do some market research and market testing before you invest too much in the business. Take a look at chapter 6 for some guidance. Nevertheless, if you are offering a service that doesn't require premises you may just start promoting your offer to see if people will buy. It's the best form of market research you can do! Do make sure that you have checked out the legal considerations first, see chapter 5.

The big advantage of starting a business from scratch is that you can design the business according to your own vision and your 'why'. You don't have to follow anyone else's guidelines or keep any existing customers happy. However, you would be well advised to test out your ideas on your ideal customers and to listen to professional expertise before spending too much money. Whilst you should listen to guidance, following it is optional. Use it to question your ideas, to test out options and to add a sanity check before your enthusiasm runs away with you. Ultimately, you must make your own decisions so that your business has its points of difference that will make it stand out from the crowd.

Starting without all the answers...

*Successful barrister **Lucy Pitts** found herself at a bit of a crossroads following the birth of her three children in fairly swift succession. Originally thinking she would go back to law she soon realised that wasn't going to work, but what next? Lucy admits that she had lost her identity in what she calls her 'defrosting period'. As a barrister she was used to being self-employed but didn't feel she had many transferable skills. After experimenting with a couple of options she decided to investigate writing, something she had enjoyed as a teenager. She undertook a diploma in copywriting and her new business was born. Although her business didn't derive from a great 'why' she now delights in being able to help small businesses grow.*

Lucy admits that she didn't have everything fully thought through when she started her business. She didn't have a clear route to market or target audience but she did have a website, a Facebook page and some networking contacts, so she started. She assumed that would be enough to win business and has been a bit surprised that winning business actually involves selling! She confesses that she has a newfound appreciation of the contribution her barrister's clerk made to her earlier self-employed career. She describes her journey as a steep and continuing learning curve but recognises that this is part of being an entrepreneur.

Is running a business right for you?

Not everyone is cut out to run a business. It can be demanding, time consuming, disappointing, frustrating and dull. It can also be exhilarating, rewarding, challenging and fun. Many owners of small businesses find themselves working longer and more unsocial hours in the constant struggle to keep on top of everything. They find themselves bogged down in administration and management when they would rather be delivering for clients. Self-doubt, procrastination and overwhelm are the scourge of many a small business owner.

It isn't all bad of course. The rewards can be many and varied, not just financial. Making an impact, customer satisfaction and personal development are just some of the non-financial rewards that the entrepreneur might look forward to.

Running a business can be lonely. Who do you share decision making with? Who do you bounce ideas around with? Who will share the anxieties? Who will share your success? I remember winning a very big contract fairly early on in my business and bouncing home to share my success with my husband only to be greeted by a fairly unenthusiastic, 'Well done. How much is it worth?' Of course I couldn't expect my husband to see what a big deal this contract was or the amount of blood, sweat and tears that had gone into winning it.

By the age of 40 we've already acquired a lot of baggage. Will your past experiences help you or hinder you in building a business? Have you acquired lots of useful skills and interests that are just ripe for turning into a business? Or are you a little battered and bruised by some negative history, by past disappointments and by people telling you that you can't do things? Life's experiences are what make us, what forms our character and what builds our resilience. However, it's all too easy to be discouraged by things from our past so it will be important to work on your mindset and to learn from the past rather than let it rule your future.

So here are a few questions to consider before you take the leap:

- How good are you at self-motivation and keeping going when the going gets tough?
- Can you make decisions without consulting others?
- How good are you at juggling lots of different tasks?
- Are you willing to sell and promote your business and yourself?
- Are you numerate?
- Do you enjoy risk taking?
- Are you prepared to sell?

Deciding what's right for you

If you are still wavering at this point, wondering whether running a business is right for you or which idea to choose then you might find some of these decision-making tools helpful.

SWOT analysis

	Positives	**Negatives**
Internal	**Strengths** These are internal positives so will include your skills, knowledge, abilities, experience etc. For a business or supplier it will include what they are good at.	**Weaknesses** These are internal areas for improvement so will include your lack of knowledge, experience and things you find difficult. For a business they will include things they don't do well but remember, if you are taking on an existing business, weaknesses offer you an opportunity to add value so they are not always a negative.
External	**Opportunities** These are external factors which you can take advantage of but over which you have little or no control. You might consider things like changes in legislation, government funding for business support, local developments such as commercial or residential buildings.	**Threats** These are the external factors which might work against you so may also include changes in legislation, reductions in funding and environmental changes.

This is a useful, commonly used tool for weighing up decisions in all sorts of situations. You can use it to assess whether running a business is right for you or to consider a particular business opportunity, premises, suppliers and a whole lot more. The tool will allow you to compare different options too.

If you are not familiar with the tool, SWOT stands for Strengths, Weaknesses, Opportunities and Threats and the analysis is usually laid out as a grid. The beauty of this is that it gives you a very visual image to help with the decision making. When laid out correctly, as above, you have one column that shows all the positives and one showing all the negatives. One row shows the internal factors which you can control, at least to an extent, whilst the other shows all the external factors over which you have little control.

If you are weighing up several alternatives, doing a SWOT analysis for each option may make the choice relatively easy.

Scoring grid

This is another decision-making tool which you may find helpful when you are comparing various options, for example one franchise over another, or one premises in comparison with another. Here you map out the various deciding factors on one axis and the various options on the other and then score each option against each factor to arrive at a total for each option. You'll need to think about your assessment criteria, what's most important to you, for each factor.

So in our example below it is clear that Franchise B is the front runner.

Using decision-making tools as well as your intuition will help you to make a confident decision although sadly does not guarantee success. If you still need some help there are more tools and assistance in the workbook.

	Franchise A	Franchise B	Franchise C
How established is the business?	6	7	4
Feedback from existing franchisees	5	8	8
Investment required	7	6	7
Support on offer	5	8	7
Profit potential	6	8	6
Total	**29**	**37**	**32**

In summary...

- There are a range of business models you could consider depending upon your attitude to risk, the financial investment required, whether you have a business idea and your skills and experience
- Franchising, network marketing and buying an existing business may involve less risk than starting from scratch
- Network marketing may offer you the most flexibility for the least investment
- You should be able to see an opportunity for growth if you are considering buying an existing business
- Starting a business from scratch gives you the most opportunity to create a business around your own ideas but can be risky
- Running a business is not for everyone
- Decision-making tools can help you to reach a conclusion

To get you thinking...

- Do I have a clear idea for a business and a vision for how it will make money?
- Can I find a franchise or network marketing company that matches my values and sells a product or service that I really like?
- How could I add value to an existing business?
- Do I have the skills and resilience to run a business?

Action points...

- Investigate your options for starting a business
- Decide which option to pursue

Chapter **3**

Some fundamentals of business

'**What do you need to start a business? Three simple things: know your product better than anyone. Know your customer, and have a burning desire to succeed.'**
—Dave Thomas, founder of Wendy's

The key to success in business is having a product or service that enough people want to pay a high enough price for, often enough, to make a sustainable profit and to have enough cash available all the time to enable you to keep trading. The key to having the right product or service is to identify a problem that enough people want to solve to provide you with that steady stream of customers. To find that problem you really need to understand your customers.

Basic principles

You can't sell to everyone

One of the most common mistakes in business is to think you can serve everybody. You can't. Think about your own buyer behaviour, there will be some stores and supermarkets which you regularly use and others which you rarely, if ever, visit. Think about your own family: do your children buy from the same places as you or do you buy from the same places as your parents? I doubt it. We spend our money where we feel most comfortable, in the places where we feel understood. Your customers are the same. So if you try to appeal to everyone the chances are that you'll appeal to nobody! Your offer will be bland and generic and unlikely to create any customer loyalty. We'll consider how you identify your ideal customer in chapter 6.

Another common mistake is to believe that people will buy what they need. Do you? Most of us buy what we want rather than what we need. We may want what we need or we may construct a very self-persuasive argument that we need what we want. Just think what you are making do with because buying a replacement is unexciting. I'll bet you can also think of something which you've recently bought for which you didn't really have a need but which you really wanted. Your customers are just like you, they will spend their money on what they want, which is not necessarily what they need. Your challenge will be to make them want what you sell!

Will you be able to rely on repeat business?

If your product or service is something your ideal customer will want to buy on a regular basis then building a sustainable business will be relatively easy if you give your customers a great experience. It's more difficult when your service is a once in a lifetime purchase, for example wedding planning, when you will be constantly on the hunt for new customers. In this case you'll be looking for a product or service that will always be in demand albeit from different customers. For example, women will go on having babies for as long as the world exists but most won't have more than two or three. If you are supplying a service to new mums there will always be someone who wants that service but the chances are they'll be new customers. The beauty of a locally based business is that you should be able to generate more business by referral and by establishing a really good reputation in your local area.

Charge the right price

One question I always ask when I'm running start-up courses is, 'Why should people buy from you rather than a competitor?' All too frequently the answer comes back, 'We'll be cheaper.' That is a race to oblivion! The chances are that if you compete on price your more established competitors will cut their prices to retain their customers. We'll discuss pricing in more detail in chapter 9 but it is a fundamental of good business to charge a price that will allow you to make a profit. It's also important to remember that many customers buy on quality and value rather than price so there are plenty of other ways for you to compete for business.

Cash is king!

If you don't have sufficient cash to pay your bills you will be trading illegally even if your business is profitable. This is something you'll need to consider when you are working out how much finance you need to start your business. Don't be tempted to underestimate to make it less scary! We'll discuss how to calculate your requirements and your options for raising finance in chapter 9.

Work out what will make you money

As an entrepreneur you will probably have lots of different ideas for your business but they probably won't all make you money and some ideas will take longer to become profitable than others. Work out which ideas will give you the best and quickest returns for the lowest investment and risk and prioritise those.

You will need to sell

You will be very lucky if people beat a path to your door begging you to take their money! The chances are that you will need to sell or at the very least ask for the sale. If you're not prepared to do this then you will need to employ someone who is good at it. This doesn't mean that you have to go for the hard sell but you will need to help people to buy or convert enquiries into sales. If this is not something you are experienced in there are lots of courses and workshops that can help.

Business planning

There's an oft-quoted saying, 'Failure to plan is planning to fail'. I'll hold my hands up here; when I started my business I didn't have a fully developed plan. I was working on one when I was offered two pieces of work and the offers kept coming in so I kept busy but it meant that I was in 'busyness' not business. I said yes to everything. A business plan would have helped me to be more strategic in my decision making. Before you ask, I do have one now!

The type of business plan you produce will depend upon what you want it for. If you want to raise finance you will need a fully developed, professional-looking, plan. However, if your plan is to help you to make the right decisions to grow your business it doesn't need to be anything fancy, a sheet of A4 or some jottings in a notebook may well suffice. If you work your way through the workbook that accompanies this book you will have a plan that should meet your needs. The following questions cover many of the issues your plan will need to address:

- What am I selling? Think solutions to problems and the results your customers can expect rather than products and services. Products and services come later
- Who is my ideal customer?
- How would my ideal customer recognise the need for my services?

- What alternative solutions might my prospect consider?
- Where would my ideal customer look to find a solution to their problem?
- How often would my ideal customer have a desire for my product or service?
- How much would my ideal customer be prepared to pay?
- Where will I source supplies? How long will it take from order to delivery? How much will they cost? What taxes or duties will be payable?
- How reliable are the sources of supply?
- Where will I trade from? How much will that cost? Are there any legal requirements about trading from there that I need to consider?
- What other legislation might impact on my business? How will I ensure that I comply? Where can I get up to date advice?
- How will my ideal customer find out about my services (i.e. your marketing plan)?
- How will I manage every aspect of my business? Think about buying, selling, marketing, finance, invoicing, administration, service delivery, cleaning etc. How will you find any help you need?
- How will my business make money?
- What's my pricing strategy?
- What seasonal variations should I expect in the demand for my services?
- What's the time lag between me spending money on supplies and receiving the cash from sales?
- What costs do I need to account for? How much will they be and when are they payable?
- What is my break-even point?
- What's my ultimate aim for the business and what are my short-, medium- and long-term goals?

We'll address these questions in later chapters and the financial plans that you will need to complete.

A working document...

Jane Hardy is one of those who did have a business plan from the word go. This is what she has to say about business planning:

'A business plan is a movable feast. Keep it under review and be prepared to adapt to circumstances. It's important to keep an eye on the numbers, to set budgets and stick to them and to measure results.'

Jane's planning tips:

- *Look for the ideas that will make you money*
- *Don't get distracted by ideas that will not make money*
- *Things will always take longer and cost more than you expect*

What problems should you be prepared for?

It would be disingenuous of me to suggest that you won't encounter doubts, opposition and problems as you launch your business but forewarned is forearmed so what should you think about?

Lack of support from family and friends

Be prepared for the critics and the naysayers for there will be some. You may even find them very close to home. Usually your friends and family will be trying to protect you from hurt and disappointment but unless they have directly relevant experience to base their criticisms on don't give them too much headroom.

Of course you will want the support of your partner and family especially if you are risking the family home or lifestyle. They may be right that returning to paid employment would be the safer option but will it give you the rewards you seek, both emotional and financial? You will need to marshal your arguments to gain their support. A sound business plan will help, as will examples of people who have transformed their family circumstances as a result of success in business.

Self-doubt

There will almost certainly be times when you doubt the wisdom of your venture. Expect it. Build a tribe of like-minded entrepreneurs who understand the ups and downs of running a business. A networking group can help and there are numerous social media groups that exist to help people to start and grow a business, there's even one associated with this book: https://www.facebook.com/groups/Foundedafter40/

A common problem...

Many of my interviewees, especially the women, admitted to self-doubt and a lack of self-confidence. For most this impacted the way they set their prices as they questioned their value so tended to under-price. However, they all report that their self-confidence has grown with their businesses and they now feel able to charge a more realistic price. Many credit networking for boosting their self-confidence, partly through having to make a pitch for business but also because they meet other people like them and some who are even less confident than they are!

Never enough time

You may be starting a business now that your family is becoming more independent leaving you with a lack of purpose and time on your hands. Of course your life may be busy with family, home, voluntary activities and your social life and you're wondering how you will ever find time to run a business. Whether you currently have too much or too little time, once you start a business the chances are that you will struggle to find time for everything you need to do. We'll consider how you deal with this challenge in the next chapter.

Another common problem:

This was another issue cited by the majority of my interviewees. Most own up to working in the evening and at weekends and some even work whilst on holiday. This isn't always driven by a business need though. Some are so enthusiastic about developing their businesses that they choose to work even in what should be downtime.

Lack of customers

Winning customers can take time and is certainly something you'll have to work at. Your marketing plan will need to outline strategies for raising awareness amongst potential clients, for converting prospects into customers and for securing repeat business and referrals from your happy buyers. We'll consider some of the options in chapter 11.

It will take longer than you think...

Most interviewees found that it took longer to bring customers through the door than they imagined. This is probably more prevalent when the business owner is unclear about their target market and/or when the purchase is relatively high value.

Too much business

Maybe you think this isn't a problem but too much business can find you under-delivering on your promises, stretching your cash flow to breaking point and working excessive hours. Take care that you don't over commit. Sometimes the right decision is to turn work away or to be clear that there will be a delay before you can do the work. It's very tempting to say yes to everything but unless you can bring in help to deliver on your promises the right answer is no. Remember that as a local business your reputation is everything so protect it by keeping your promises.

People asking for freebies

The chances are that there will be friends and family members who want what you are selling but don't expect to pay full or, sometimes, any price. You will need to think how you will deal with these. On the one hand friends and family can be good for referrals and testimonials but if they don't pay the going rate they are bad for profits and can take up time that would be better spent building your business.

You will need to make it clear that this is now your business and that you will need to charge at least 'mates rates' and that friends and family will come behind genuine customers in the queue for your time unless they are paying full price. Perhaps you can offer a discount for each new customer a friend or family member introduces or maybe you could trade skills for help you need. Whatever you decide, be consistent to avoid being dragged into arguments.

Lack of cash

Cash flow or the lack of it can be the cause of anxiety and stress for many business owners. You will need to keep a close eye on your finances at least until you have built up sufficient reserves to support your business. Be realistic, even pessimistic, in your cash flow projections and try to have a contingency plan if you do find yourself short. Credit card debts are very expensive so think about negotiating loans or overdrafts to tide you over a tricky patch.

People turning on you

Sadly not everyone will wish you success. You may find some people will deliberately sabotage your efforts and sometimes you will be let down by people you thought you could trust. Be careful what you give people access to and make sure that you change passwords, locks and access promptly if someone betrays your trust. Minimise the risks by monitoring contributions carefully and by building in regular progress checks.

Life will get in the way!

We don't run our businesses in a vacuum and sometimes life puts a spanner in the works. Our own illness or that of a family member can take us away from our businesses. Children or parents may need additional support when you least expect it. The car will break down or there'll be a transport strike on a day when you need to travel to an important meeting. Sometimes we'll be able to make adjustments or alternative arrangements but other times we just have to accept that there are circumstances beyond our control and do what we can to minimise the consequences. This is why it is so helpful to have a support team who can step in to help when needed. These might be people you outsource to, people in your network or family members. Having your systems and processes documented will make it easier for people to step in in the event of an emergency.

Family comes first...

*When **Jane Hardy** bought her business in early 2014 her elderly mother was fit and well and very independent. A few months later, after a fall and the onset of dementia, Jane found herself spending increasing amounts of time looking after her mum's welfare. Fortunately, Jane had a couple of people on her team who could step in to help but it also made Jane realise that she had to structure the business so that it was less dependent on her all the time.*

In summary...

- You will need to be clear about who you are selling to and how much repeat business you can expect
- You'll need to work out what will make you money, charge the right price for it and ensure that your business has sufficient cash available at all times to enable you to keep trading
- A business plan will give you a route map to follow in the early stages of your business and help you to anticipate problems before you start
- There are a number of problems that you should be prepared for including lack of customers and cash, people letting you down and life getting in the way

To get you thinking...

- How will your business idea make money?
- What could get in the way of you being able to focus on your business as much as you want or need to? How can you minimise the risk that distractions might have on your business?

Action points...

- Start thinking about what you will sell and to whom, which we'll cover in more detail in chapter 6

Chapter **4**

Finding time for your business

'You will never find time for anything. If you want time
you must make it.'

—**Charles Buxton**

As we've already seen, having enough time for every aspect
of running a successful business whilst also having a life is a
challenge. The first thing we have to accept as business owners is
that there will always be things on the 'to do' list. Our goal must
therefore be to ensure that we get our priorities done whilst also
making space for downtime.

Our clients and customers will inevitably be high on our
priority list but the danger is that they can suck all our time so
that we spend all our days working *in* our businesses and no time
working *on* them. This is dangerous because without marketing
we'll eventually run out of customers, without invoicing we will
run out of money and without record keeping completing our tax
returns will be a nightmare! Not to mention ordering supplies,
planning, personal development, recruitment, staff training and
all the other tasks that go into running a business. It is therefore

vital that we make time for working *on* our businesses. In this chapter I'll share some tips, tools and techniques that some fellow business owners and I have found useful.

Avoid bright shiny objects

Bright shiny objects are the curse of most business owners. Bright shiny objects are often disguised as moneymaking ideas, a new bit of kit that might transform our businesses or an exciting but ethereal lead. Now I'm not saying that we should dismiss ideas, new kit or potential leads but we need to ensure that they don't distract us from our priorities. I see too many business owners pursuing endless ideas and never landing any so their businesses struggle to grow or even survive.

Most of these bright shiny objects quickly lose their sparkle so design a system that allows you to capture the ideas but to park them for a while, a notebook or a file on your computer perhaps. Revisit the ideas in time that you have set aside for business development and see if they are still as attractive, if they are, schedule time for research and development.

Many of the most successful business people describe focus as a key factor in their success. They don't allow themselves to be distracted by bright shiny objects.

Focus, focus, focus...

*When she started her life coaching business **Monica Castenetto** had lots of ideas but wasn't sure which would work so she did a lot of experimenting. She ended up 'swamped and overwhelmed'. It was when she began to see – and measure – her results that she got a feel for what was working and was able to let go of things that weren't. She also cut out activities and services that were taking too much time and energy for the rewards they generated.*

> *Now Monica introduces just one new idea at a time and waits until she can see the results before she introduces anything else. And she has learned to say no to projects and opportunities that take her too far off her focus.*

Establish priorities

Your clients will dictate some of your priorities but others should come from your business plan. Your business plan is something that you should be referring to all the time, if you're not, the chances are the plan is not suitable for your needs or you are working on things that are not important.

Marketing

For any business the number one priority must be to win and retain profitable customers. This means that marketing must be something you pay regular attention to. What tends to happen in many businesses is that they turn on the marketing tap, which splutters a bit but eventually leads to a stream of business. Serving the needs of those customers takes all the business' time so they turn off the marketing tap only to find a while later that there are no more customers in the pipeline and the process has to start again. This means that the business experiences constant peaks and troughs, which is stressful and has a negative effect on profits. Making time for regular marketing should therefore be a priority for every business but if you don't have the time or skill to do it yourself it is one of those activities that you can largely outsource.

Business development

Business development should always be a priority. It's important to be aware of developments in your line of work so that you can take advantage of new opportunities and take action to deal with any threats.

We live in an incredibly fast-moving world, which is both a blessing and a curse. It has not been that long since Apple launched the iPad. At the time, journalists and others expressed doubts as to the commercial validity of the idea but others embraced the possibilities and Apple sold 19 million in the first year. What's more, the iPad has spawned numerous businesses designing apps to enable purchasers to make best use of their device. Competitors had to play catch up designing tablets of their own and sales of laptop computers experienced a period of steady decline. The iPad and its competitors created opportunities that small businesses were able to take advantage of, either by designing an iPad-based product, or by using the iPad to deliver services in a different way. For example, conference organisers are issuing iPads to delegates to enable them to access the presentations, take notes and vote on key issues. At the end of the event the attendees return the iPads and their personal record of the event is emailed to them. On a recent visit to Budapest I was shown the dishes on the menu on an iPad so language was no barrier. Nurseries and schools are using iPads to record children's activities allowing parents to see what their little ones are doing during the day. The iPad has proved a differentiator to businesses that have spotted and embraced its potential but it may be past its peak as smartphones become ever more sophisticated and laptops are reinvented to take on some of the tablet functionality.

But new technologies can destroy a business. Some years ago I worked with an entrepreneur who thought his future was made. He had invested in a machine that managed video lending through a hole in the wall, his customers would be able to rent and return a video at whatever time of the day or night suited them. He thought his main competitor was Blockbuster. What he didn't anticipate was live streaming that would allow Netflix and their rivals to deliver films and programmes to people's home at the click of a mouse.

So make sure that one of your priorities is looking for the opportunities and for threats to your business both locally and more widely. Other priorities will be personal to your business and individual goals. It's important to schedule specific time for these.

Managing your priorities

The chances are you will have a million and one things on your to-do list and if you try to keep them in your head you are bound to forget something. You may favour paper to-do lists but they tend to need a lot of rewriting and updating. There's a vast array of web-based tools that can help, many of them have a free or low cost version that is adequate for the start-up business owner. I suggest that you try some of them out until you find the one that works best for you. See the website www.foundedafter40.co.uk for some suggestions.

Busy business owners' tips for getting things done...

Lucy Pitts is an advocate of time blocking for getting things done and she's also a list maker. She starts each week with a list of the tasks she has to complete and adds to it as the work comes in. Her days have a regular pattern allowing time for work and for getting the children to and from school and walking the dogs. She frequently returns to her desk once the children are in bed and will use the weekends to mop up any unfinished tasks, she also admits to working whilst on holiday, especially at the start of a break.

Giles Button worked 100 hours a week for 5 years before he accepted that more hours don't always mean more productivity and that the opposite can be true. He believes that whilst you have to work hard and be flexible it's also important to have a balance and take a break. For him that means playing sport, which really helps him to switch off.

Leonie Wright gets a lot done; she attributes this to organisation and time management. Leonie is an advocate of time blocking and usually works in two-hour blocks of time, which she schedules in her paper diary, 'it's so much easier to see your commitments in a paper diary,' says Leonie. Leonie does a lot of networking and makes a point of scheduling meetings after an event to cut down on travel time. She also uses time in the car, when she's not driving, to catch up, especially with emails. She's an advocate of switching off emails to focus on development work and allocates three to four hours a week to working on her business' development.

Avoid procrastination and perfectionism

I wish I had £1 for every would-be entrepreneur that I've worked with who has been waiting until they'd put just one more piece in the jigsaw before launching their business! Research, training, family, trading name and brand identity are just some of the excuses I regularly hear. Let me tell you, you will never be totally prepared for starting your business. There will always be more you could understand about your target market, about potential suppliers and your competition but you have to draw a line somewhere. There will always be things you need to learn but you can learn on the job, or buy in the skills until you are confident in your own abilities. Your family will always want some of you; it's just the nature of the demands that change. You can always change your trading name if you've really got it wrong and you can develop your brand identity as you go. So watch out for the excuses you are making for not starting. Ask yourself whether you are procrastinating or being guilty of perfectionism. Procrastination and perfectionism are huge time thieves.

Perfection doesn't exist! Excellence is good enough. Good is better than many. Strive for excellence and even if you fall a little short your offer will be good enough. Be prepared to learn and to improve. Own up if things go wrong and put them right.

The very best research comes from trying to sell your product or service. Learning done on the job tends to stick. Families tend to adapt to changing circumstances. Stop making excuses and start! You don't have to start with a big song and dance. You can do a soft launch where you simply open your doors, metaphorically or literally. Start trading quietly. Market your business on a small scale so you can learn as you go. Hopefully the momentum will soon build but if things aren't quite right you'll be able to make the changes without major impact on your business.

 The best way to avoid procrastination (and in my experience perfectionism can be a form of procrastination) is to set a start date and share it with people who will hold you accountable. This is where it's helpful to have a coach, mentor or mastermind group who will support you on your journey and challenge you to meet your goals. Agree your deadline and your milestones with your support network and stick to them.

The Power Hour

I have to thank Carrie Wilkerson, aka The Barefoot Executive, for introducing me to the power hour. It's my favourite tool for getting things done. The idea is that you dedicate an hour, usually the first of the day, to working *on* your business. Do this before you check emails, social media or open the post so that you are working on your own agenda and not other people's. Set a timer (smartphones are useful for this) for one hour (or 20 minutes if you are really pushed for time) and be clear what you want to achieve in that time. When the timer goes off make a note of what you need to do next and put the work away ready for your next power hour. That's the hard bit! Once you've created the momentum it's hard to stop; if you don't have other priorities of course you can keep going.

If you can do a power hour five days a week for 48 weeks of the year you will have created the equivalent of six weeks' worth of average working hours to work on your business' development. Think what you could achieve in six weeks of work on your business. Even if you can only manage 20 minutes a day you would create the equivalent of two weeks' worth of business development.

Automating tasks

Repetitive tasks can take a great deal of time but these days many can be automated. For example, most computer-based accountancy packages will allow you to automate repeating invoices. Other tools allow you to upload your receipts into your accounting package via your smartphone, email or post. No more time wasted hunting for paper receipts or typing the details into your accounts and filing.

Spend a few hours of your business development time preparing your marketing materials and then schedule delivery of emails using tools like mailchimp.com, convertkit.com, constantcontact.com and others according to your needs and budget. Tools like hootsuite.com, buffer.com and Facebook's own scheduling tool will allow you to programme social media broadcast posts for the future.

If booking appointments is vital to your business then there's a huge array of tools available to allow clients to book themselves in. You can programme different types of availability into diary management programmes like acuityscheduling.com, calendly. com, appointy.com and many more. Many of these programmes work with payment processors like PayPal to enable a client to pay before the appointment so reducing the number of no-shows.

If you run events then programmes like Eventbrite.com and bookingbug.com offer an integrated service that allows you to send marketing emails, take bookings and payments, send tickets, print attendee lists and name badges etc.

All of this can save a huge amount of time and money and the programmes are often very reasonably priced. Some take a percentage of fees processed rather than a monthly or annual charge. It's well worth taking some time to investigate software that is specifically designed for your industry as there is an enormous amount available to suit all budgets.

 If you can automate routine and repetitive tasks you should be able to make time for the things that really need your attention.

Getting help

It's tempting to think that we need to do everything ourselves when we're just starting out. We convince ourselves that it's easier to do it than to explain what we want done to someone else. We think no one else can do a job as well as we can. We believe that we can't afford to pay for assistance. However, the time we spend on tasks that do not generate income can actually cost us so it is worth considering bringing in some help.

Giles Button on outsourcing...

'A mentor once taught me a great expression, "Only do what only you can do". I made the mistake of doing everything that I could, especially the IT. Whilst this appeared to save money it took away a lot of time and often negatively affected productivity. I found it was best to look for systems that I could use and outsource where possible. I resisted outsourcing for a long time, but it was a much more flexible model.

I'd highly recommend having everything electronic and "in the cloud". This really helped me work smartly, working on the go and not being worried if systems went down.'

Invoicing, bookkeeping, administration, marketing, sales, design and manufacture are just some of the things you can outsource to others leaving you to work on building your business. The internet has made it possible to secure much of this help from anywhere in the world. Programmes like peopleperhour. com and fiverr.com allow you to recruit help on a project basis often very cheaply. Do your due diligence though and check out the reputation of the people you are outsourcing to. Look at some of their work. What do the reviewers say about them? How does your gut instinct feel?

Networking events can be an excellent way to find locally based help from self-employed virtual assistants, bookkeepers, marketers etc. Using someone with local knowledge can also have its advantages for a locally based business as your assistant may have useful contacts and ideas that would help grow your business.

When bringing in help it's important to devote time to communication and training so that your assistant knows exactly what they are meant to do, how your systems work and how you like to operate. It's therefore helpful to build a relationship that can be ongoing so that you are not constantly training someone new. For that reason you may consider recruiting employees to meet your needs. Before you go down this route think about your legal commitments and the full range of costs including pay rates, taxation, insurance and pensions. You will also need to generate a number of policies and procedures to protect both you and your employee. Chapter 12 covers this topic in much more detail.

Creating work-life balance

Many business owners struggle to achieve the work-life balance that they craved when they started their businesses. Whilst they have been able to schedule time out for the kids' graduation ceremonies or some voluntary work it's usually at the expense of some very early mornings or late nights. Managing the balance requires discipline and a willingness to set parameters and even to say no on occasion.

Monica Castenetto's life balance tips...

Monica's business is called 'Live a Life You Love' so to her it's really important to do just that and create space for all the non-work activities that give her life balance and joy.

- Plan in the non-business things you really want to do first and well in advance – then let the business commitments and activities flow around them
- Set work time rules and stick to them. Close the office door when it's not work time and stay out
- Schedule longer breaks to give yourself chance to recharge your batteries
- Book yourself onto non-work activities you enjoy – either with friends and family, or through a course. You book it, you pay for it, you commit to it – so you'll have a stronger incentive to stop working and turn up for it!

In summary...

- Avoid distractions and focus on what you know will move your business forward
- Establish and manage your priorities using time management techniques that work for you
- Don't wait for everything to be perfect. Look out for the excuses you are making for not taking action
- Automate or outsource tasks where you can
- Decide what your ideal work-life balance looks like and manage your diary to achieve it

To get you thinking...

- What does your ideal work-life balance look like?
- What comes easily to you and what could be better done by someone else?
- What hours will you need to trade to meet your customers' expectations? Will you need to bring in some help if you are to trade these hours without exhausting yourself?

Action points...

- Set a date for launching your business (or if it's too early for that, set a date by which you will make a decision on how or what you will launch)
- Investigate time management, automation and outsourcing options for your business and how much they will cost you. The tools described in this chapter are only some of those available and there are always new options entering the marketplace
- Book some downtime into your diary

Part **2**

Developing the plan

Chapter **5**

Legal considerations

'Ignorance of the law excuses no man from practicing it.'
—**Addison Mizner**

Every business needs to trade within the law. Failure to do so can lead to catastrophic damage to a business' reputation, not to mention the time and money spent on legal cases. I am not a lawyer, the law is different in each jurisdiction and changes are frequent so all I intend to do in this chapter is to encourage you to think where legislation might impact your business and to take proper advice to ensure you are trading legally. I have given links to websites where further guidance is available as these can change. Please check the website www.foundedafter40.co.uk for current links.

This is not the most exciting part of setting up a business so you may wish to skip this chapter for now but do come back to it when you're ready because it is important.

Your trading status

 You will need to choose an appropriate trading status for your business. Your decision will probably be based on the people involved in the business, the degree of risk involved and your need for finance. In the UK you can change your trading status as the business develops.

You will need to inform the tax office when you start trading but other registrations will depend upon the nature of your business. Setting up a company is not always the right decision so consult an accountant or business adviser before you make your final decision. The following is a brief overview of your options; you can find more detailed guidance at www.gov.uk:

- *Sole trader:* the law does not recognise a difference between you and the business so you are liable for any business debts but can keep the profits after paying the appropriate taxes. You can still employ staff as a sole trader.
- *Partnership:* two or more people own the business. The partners would be 'jointly and severally liable'. This means that one partner can make a decision or commitment on behalf of all the other partners, which all the partners would then be liable for. In a worst case scenario a partner could disappear leaving the remaining partners with all of the commitments and debts, including the absent partner's share. If you are considering a partnership, even with your life partner, please get a qualified lawyer to draw up a legal partnership agreement.
- *Limited liability partnership:* the partners own the business but there are protections in place against negligence and misconduct by other partners. A limited liability partnership must be registered with Companies House and operate within its guidelines. Partners may

share profits. You will need to file annual returns with Companies House.

- *Limited company:* the shareholders own the company and you would be an employee. You can be the sole shareholder should you choose. Profits would be retained in the business with a proportion shared amongst the shareholders. If you want to raise finance, selling shares in the business is one of the best ways to do it but you will need to have advice on the valuation of your company. Take care not to sell so many shares that you lose control of your own business. You will need to file annual returns with Companies House and some of this information will be publicly available.

Registrations and licences

In the UK only certain types of businesses need to be registered or licensed, but this is a complicated area that can vary between local authorities. In general food-related businesses need to be registered, as do some types of beauty businesses. Licences are required for the sale of certain products such as alcohol and for certain professions such as some medical and therapy services and for some activities such as events open to the public. There is a search facility on the www.gov.uk website which should tell you what action you need to take.

Protecting your assets

Does your business produce original work such as designs, artwork and writing? You should consider how best to protect your work. This may be as simple as putting the copyright symbol – © – and the year of creation on the document or it may be more involved. For instance, if you need to share your idea or design with someone else, perhaps a business adviser or manufacturer, there are legal agreements you should both sign before revealing any confidential information.

ACID – Anti Copying in Design – have a range of legal documents that may be suitable for your needs and they can signpost the advice and guidance you need. Find them at www.acid.uk.com. You can also find advice at www.own-it.org.

You may also want to trademark your name, brand names or logos or protect an invention. Whilst this can be both time consuming and expensive it is something you should consider. Search for Intellectual Property at www.gov.uk for information relevant to your business.

Health and safety

Protecting the health and safety of yourself, your staff, customers and suppliers should be something that you want to do and not just something you do because it is required by law. You will, however, need to ensure that you are aware of how health and safety legislation impacts your business.

 What kind of risk assessments will you have to do? How will you mitigate the risks identified? What health and safety training do you and your people need? For example, if you move stock or lift people you will need to ensure all concerned are trained in safe manual handling. If anyone is working from height or using certain types of equipment they may need specific training and there may be age restrictions on who can do the work. You will need to take steps to prevent slips and trips, some of the major causes of injury in work and other places.

Do you use chemicals of any kind or have people working in vulnerable areas such as cold rooms? You may need to provide protective clothing or equipment and keep safety data information as well as ensuring that your team is adequately trained.

You will need to be aware of requirements for first aid equipment and trained personnel and ensure that you display appropriate health and safety signs and notices. You should also be aware that the application of health and safety legislation changes as a business grows and takes on more employees.

Even if you work from home you will need to consider your health and safety. Is your workstation properly set up to avoid the risk of repetitive strain injuries? Is your equipment properly maintained? Do you wear sensible protective footwear or clothing when you should for your own safety? It's all too easy to cut corners when we work from home. We think of our homes as places of safety but we are often juggling business and the domestic chores, which can lead to shortcuts and accidents. Make sure that you do your risk assessments, take advice on setting up your workstation correctly and take time to work safely.

Employment law

Minimum wage, working time regulations, leave entitlements, equal opportunities, diversity, young workers, expectant and new mothers, grievance and discipline are just some of the things covered by employment law. If you employ people, even on a casual basis, you will need to ensure that you understand and comply with the law. Changes in pensions legislation will impact on every business.

You will need to give your employees a written statement of their terms of employment and access to a staff handbook outlining entitlements and policies and procedures. It's wise to seek guidance from an HR professional or employment lawyer before you take on an employee. This is an area that is ripe for outsourcing. Getting your policies and procedures right could save you a lot of time and money if things should go wrong. Make sure that you follow those procedures and take professional advice before you take drastic action such as dismissing an employee, even for something that appears to be indisputable. It is often the failure to follow a procedure, rather than an unfair decision, that costs employers when a dispute goes to court.

You will find useful guidance on employment issues at www. acas.org.uk. If you are looking for professional guidance check your networks for an HR consultant or contact www.cipd.co.uk.

If you are intending to outsource work you will need to check that your provider is registered as self-employed for tax purposes or has a limited company. You will also need to check that your contract meets the tests for self-employment. In the UK this is known as IR 35. To be considered as self-employed the individual has to meet a number of thresholds relating to the degree of control they have over the work to be done, where and when it is done and the remuneration. You can find guidance at 'www.hmrc.gov.uk.

Trading regulations

This is another hugely complicated legal area and you will need to research how the legislation applies to your particular business. Do your premises need to be checked by the fire authorities or environmental health before you can start trading? Do your staff need to be checked for criminal convictions? Do you need to be licensed or hold a particular qualification for the work you intend to do? What about guarantees, standards of work and refunds?

Do you have the right to sell the branded merchandise you have bought wholesale? Can you incorporate someone else's design or character in your work? It may seem very tempting to develop a design based on the latest blockbuster movie but unless you have obtained a licence to do so you are likely to find yourself in a legal dispute. Businesses large and small should be fiercely protective of their intellectual property so using someone else's idea without their specific, written permission is a bad idea. Don't assume that you are safe because you are a tiny business in the UK borrowing a theme from a business on the other side of the world; you are not.

Whilst trading regulations are many and various they do tend to be based on fairness for both the business and the consumer. Put yourself in the consumer's shoes, how would you like to be treated? If you treat your customers as you would like to be treated you will probably be within the law, but it's still important to check. Think how you would feel if another business adapted your design, idea or creative work, and don't treat others in a way you would not be happy with, even if they are big corporations.

Remember that the law is there to protect you and your business too. This means that you could have redress when you are treated unfairly. Be prepared to fight for what is rightfully yours especially if someone else's behaviour is adversely affecting your business. Protect your business by having clear terms and conditions that are right for your business. Don't be tempted to take someone else's document from the internet, that is copyright theft and the terms may not be suitable for your business. Ensure that your terms state which country's law applies.

Getting help...

Alastair Lyon is an independent financial adviser; his is a highly regulated industry. In order to make sure he's operating correctly Alastair pays into a compliance service that makes sure that he's up to date with the law and the regulatory framework. This service includes an annual compliance check, which covers his systems, records, correspondence and advice. This means that Alastair is prepared when his business is the subject of an official compliance check.

Managing data and communications

Yours might be a locally based business but you should have a website and will probably store customer and other information on a computer or 'in the cloud'. You will therefore need to comply with the relevant legislation e.g. The Data Protection Act.

This means thinking about what data you really need to collect, how long you need to keep it and how you will do so securely. There are strict rules in a great deal of countries about how you can share data and with whom. You will also need to think about how you gather data, especially personal information and ensure that the data owners give you permission to use it in the way you intend to. For instance, if you go to a networking event at which business cards are exchanged it doesn't automatically mean that you can add all those names to your mailing list. You will probably need to have specific permission.

Unless a person has opted in to your list you will need to check their contact information against opt-out lists such as the telephone preference service to ensure that you are not contacting people illegally. The potential fines are huge.

Check what specific information, statements and policies you need to display on your website. For example, you will need to display a mailing address and a cookie policy (a cookie is a small piece of code placed on a website to track visitor behaviour).

Taxation

Which taxes apply to your business will depend upon your trading status, what you sell, where you sell and your turnover as well as the employment status of anyone who works for you. You will need to pay the taxes you owe but should manage your finances so that you don't pay any more than that. You may therefore wish to consult with an accountant to ensure that you organise your business in a way to minimise the impact of taxation on your profits.

An accountant should be able to advise you which expenses are tax deductible, and which are not, but the tax office also offer regular training webinars to owners of small businesses and self-employed people. Recordings or previous webinars may be available. Search 'webinars' at www.hmrc.gov.uk. You can also sign up for regular update emails from Her Majesty's Revenue and Customs to ensure that you stay up to date.

Insurance

There may be some forms of insurance such as public liability and employers' liability that are a legal requirement. Other insurances may give you peace of mind, for instance professional indemnity or key worker insurance.

If you work from home or deliver goods using your family car don't assume that you are covered by your home or vehicle insurance. Some home insurance companies will not cover a business operating from home and you may find your car insurance doesn't cover you if you are using it for work. It's always wise to check. You don't want to find your claim is turned down because you hadn't been open with your insurance company.

You may be able to get sound advice and competitive quotes through a trade association or a small business group. These organisations are often able to negotiate excellent, tailor-made, deals with insurers on behalf of their members and the savings you make could cover your membership fees. If you are not a member of a business group consider getting advice from an insurance broker. You will need to discuss the nature of your work, who you serve, your turnover and the size of your contracts so that the broker can assess the risks properly and give you the right advice. You will have to make a decision about which insurance to buy based on the costs, your budget and the risks involved. For instance, you might like to buy insurance to cover you if you are ill and unable to work but you might find the cost prohibitive.

It's a good idea to get a number of competitive quotes for any insurance you require so that you can be sure you are paying the right price. Sometimes buying all the different insurances you need as a bundle can save you money.

In summary...

- You will need to choose a legal entity that will be right for you and your business
- Some kinds of business need to be licensed or registered, will yours?
- The law allows protection for inventions, original products, designs or ideas
- Managing health and safety is good practice as well as a legal requirement
- There's a raft of constantly changing employment law which you will need to comply with if you employ anyone else in your business

- Different trading regulations apply to different types of business so you will need to investigate which are relevant to you
- There are strict laws governing communication and the data that you hold about other people
- Which taxes you pay will depend upon your trading status, turnover and profits. An accountant or tax adviser might be able to save you money
- Some insurances are reassuring, some are a legal requirement.

To get you thinking...

- Do you have some original designs, ideas or products that are valuable to you and your business and which you should protect against copying?
- If you plan to recruit help in your business can you offer the flexibility to meet the self-employment test?
- Will you hold data that requires you to register with www. ico.org.uk?
- What insurances will you need or want?

Action points...

- Decide upon your trading status
- Investigate whether your business will need a licence or to register with the local authority or other body
- Conduct a health and safety risk assessment for yourself and any others working on your behalf and take steps to minimise risks
- Investigate relevant trading regulations and employment law
- Get insurance quotes

Chapter **6**

Understanding your target market

'The aim of marketing is to know and understand the customer so well the product or service fits him and sells itself.'

—Peter Drucker

As we discussed in chapter 3 no business can sell to everyone though many make the mistake of trying. It may feel counter-intuitive to restrict the market you intend to supply but if you can find a niche that is narrow but deep you will make it easy for enough people to recognise themselves as your potential customers. This has advantages for the way you design and market your offer. If you have an in-depth understanding of your target customer you will understand the problems they have and want to solve. This means that you will know what products and services will appeal to them and you will be able to market them using language which is familiar to your ideal customer. If you can find a niche that your competitors are not targeting so precisely you may have a competitive advantage.

What is a narrow and deep niche?

You could target women who are mothers; that would be a niche but a wide one. If you target new mothers with babies under three months old that would be a narrow niche because it is very tightly defined but it's also a deep niche as lots of women have babies each year (around 700,000 annually in the UK). How you define your niche will depend upon the services you are offering and where you are located. For example, if you are a photographer in a major conurbation you may well be able to specialise in taking photos of newborns but if your business is based in a lightly populated rural area you may need a wider target.

Niches don't just apply to the consumer market. You should apply the same principles to business to business services. Business buyers like to purchase from suppliers who really understand their businesses. A restaurant owner wants an accountant who understands the restaurant trade and who gets why it is important to differentiate between bar and restaurant purchases for instance. An accountant who deals in small businesses in general may not have the degree of understanding to help the business owner recognise whether their costs are adequately controlled and in line with the most profitable businesses in their sector.

How do I find the right niche?

In the ideal world your business idea and your *'why'* will have been born out of the identification of a problem that enough people want to solve with a solution exclusive to you. Sadly few of us live in an ideal world so your *'why'* may be the starting point for defining your target customer.

 If your *'why'* isn't narrow enough to form a niche, list all the different types of customer you could supply. How many of each type are there in your local area? Who else is serving their needs? Are there some groups whose needs are better met than others? For instance, if you are thinking of selling clothes and your local shopping centre is filled with fashion boutiques and chain stores there may be a space for you to sell high-end classic clothes to affluent women. But of course there will need to be enough affluent women in the local area to make your business viable.

Your local authority should be able to supply you with demographic data for the local population but much of this is gathered in the population census only carried out every 10 years. Other data may be gleaned from electoral registration records, planning applications, council tax and business rate records. The local authority may have done research of their own to inform infrastructure and other development plans. Contact the department responsible for business support to see what data is available in your locality.

If there are large housing or commercial building developments happening in your area you may find that the people behind them have commissioned some research which they may be willing to share for a fee. It's also worth a visit to your local library to see what information they hold. Some Chambers of Commerce have research departments and demographic and business data so could be another source of useful information.

Make use of your own local knowledge too. What do you know about local businesses or residents? Is there anything that your neighbours struggle to find? Are there local Facebook groups that you could tap in to in order to source the information you need?

Profiling your ideal customer

The more you understand about your ideal customer the easier it will be to serve them and to communicate with them. Mothers of newborn babies have one thing in common... their new babies, but the things they don't share may be the differentiators for your business. For instance, you may design a service to new mothers with older children or maybe your target is a professional woman returning to her career after a short maternity break.

The following are some of the elements that go into creating your ideal customer's profile:

- Age
- Gender
- Marital status
- Number and age of children
- Where they live
- Home owner or renter
- Level of academic achievement
- Professional qualifications
- Work and whether it is full time/part time/self-employed etc.
- What stage of their career they are at
- Hobbies and interests
- What they read, listen to and watch
- What they care about

If your customers are other businesses the elements that make up their profile include:

- Age of the business
- What the business does
- Their customers
- Turnover
- Where they are located
- Nature of ownership e.g. sole trader, partnership, limited company or PLC
- Their routes to market
- Their decision-making process and who their decision makers are
- What stage of growth the business is at
- What trade or business organisations they belong to
- Where they advertise or promote the business
- What they care about

When you have a really clear picture of your ideal customer you will be able to work out how to approach them, the language to use in your marketing and the triggers that will prompt action. Your aim is to speak your ideal customer's language, to help them identify with a problem they want to solve and to enable them to understand that they want your solution.

Why will your ideal customer need you?

People usually buy to solve a problem. Your challenge is to identify a problem that your ideal customer not only has but also *wants* to solve. This can be more difficult for some businesses, for example those in the creative sector where the customer may not see the purchase as a solution to a problem. However, most purchases are made using both the emotional and logical parts of our brain. This is especially true for more expensive or bigger purchases so it is important to try to tap in to our ideal customer's motivation. If your ideal customer loves your offer they will want to be able to justify buying it and that means giving themselves a good reason. A solution to a problem is a good reason so how can you position the sale as a problem solver? Some motivational theory might help.

Abraham Maslow developed his hierarchy of needs in the 1940s and early 50s and, whilst his theory has been challenged by academics in the intervening years, it does give us a useful framework from which to consider our customers' motivation. If you are not familiar with the theory, Maslow suggests that we must satisfy our needs at one level before the next level motivates us. Your task is to establish the level at which your ideal customer has an unmet need. For creative and lifestyle product businesses the need is usually at the higher levels of esteem or self-actualisation where people want to feel good about themselves and to achieve their full potential.

Our needs can change over time if our circumstances alter. Take for instance a marriage breakdown. Whereas the couple may have been living comfortably motivated by higher level needs the breakdown can leave the partners without a home or with less security than they previously enjoyed. No longer will they be motivated by the need for self-fulfilment and whilst their self-esteem may have taken a bashing the need for shelter and security will take priority.

So where on the hierarchy are your ideal customers currently and what's the next step they want to take? A coach may wish to specialise in clients at one particular level, for example a relationship specialist would be helping people who may feel lonely or that they don't belong. Another coach may help with confidence building so will look for clients who have esteem needs or perhaps their ideal clients have achieved status and recognition but are still unfulfilled, in which case self-actualisation will be their motivation.

Maslow's Hierarchy of Needs

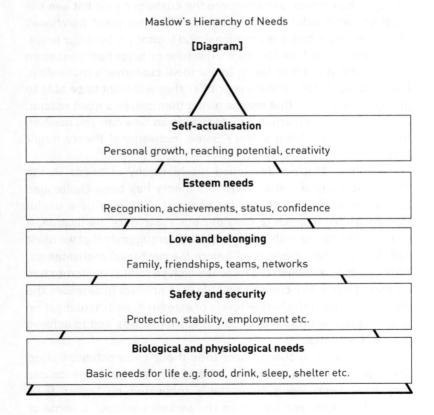

[Diagram]

Self-actualisation

Personal growth, reaching potential, creativity

Esteem needs

Recognition, achievements, status, confidence

Love and belonging

Family, friendships, teams, networks

Safety and security

Protection, stability, employment etc.

Biological and physiological needs

Basic needs for life e.g. food, drink, sleep, shelter etc.

Another way to look for problems your ideal customer wants to solve is to think about what's broken and needs fixing, or what they have too much or too little of. What's broken and needs fixing may be tangible, for instance a broken piece of equipment, or intangible such as a service that is not working properly. Your target customer may either have too little time or time on their hands, too little money or some spare cash they want to do something meaningful with. If you think about your offer and list all the different problems it can solve you can then start to research who has those problems and tie that in with your vision of your ideal client.

Time for some research

Don't be tempted to think you understand your target customer yet. At this stage you haven't tested your ideas; you may be missing something. Now is the time to do some research to establish exactly who your target customer is, why they need you and what alternative solutions they are considering.

You need to establish:
- How many people have the problem you want to solve
- Whether enough of those people find the problem irritating enough to pay for a solution
- How often they have the problem
- How much they will pay for a solution
- What kind of solution they would like to have
- What alternative providers they would consider
- If their profile matches the one you think is your ideal customer

You may not think of your business in terms of solving problems. For instance, if you design jewellery or want to open a restaurant your customers might be seeking pleasure so you want to know if they like what you will be offering. You too will need to do research to establish the likely demand and price points for your product or service.

A great fishing analogy from Gilles Pelenc...

'I often compare networking or prospecting (it works for both) to fishing:

- *If you decide one day you want to go fishing and you just go, your chances of success are better than if you stay at home, but they are not great.*
- *The moment when you decide you want to catch say a trout, then straight away you know you won't catch a trout in the middle of the ocean. Your best bet is to go to a mountain lake or even better a mountain river. So when you know your target audience, go and hover in the place where you are most likely to find them in the highest possible number.*
- *You also know that if you put a steak at the end of your rod, the trout won't bite. Trout like grasshoppers or worms. So once you know which fish to catch, you know what bait to put on the hook. Your bait is your message. Choose the right message to the right audience and you will succeed.'*

Conducting research

The problem with much research is that it tests what people think they will do rather than how they will behave so the results may give you a skewed picture. If you can find a way to test behaviour rather than opinion your research results are likely to be more accurate. This is where pop-up venues, fairs and local events can be helpful. For relatively low costs and no long-term commitment you can test whether people will buy what you offer at a price you can afford to sell at to make a profit. If producing enough stock to sell is too much of an investment can you produce enough for people to sample and then give you an opinion? Perhaps they can score your product on some key criteria or dispose of their empties in a 'would buy' or 'wouldn't buy' bin.

Try to find a way for people to give you an independent opinion. Give them a private space to fill in your questionnaire. Speak to them away from friends and family. If people have to give you their opinion surrounded by others they may be swayed by their associates and you will get the results of groupthink rather than individual opinions.

If you need to conduct a traditional market research survey be careful how you word the questions so that you are not leading your subjects towards a particular opinion. Either use a professional market research company to do the survey for you or consider using model questions designed by professional researchers. For example, www.surveymonkey.com offers you a range of market research surveys and questions that should help you get some useful answers. When you are putting yours together ask people about what they do rather than what they think. So questions like:

- How often do you buy... ?
- How much do you pay for... (rather than how much would you pay)?
- Where do you buy?

Of course there may be some questions that just have to be hypothetical but if you can limit those, the results of your survey are likely to be more useful.

Consider offering a reward to encourage more people to respond to your survey. For example when I was researching this book I offered the chance to win a £50 Amazon voucher; that really boosted the number of responses I got from a list I'd surveyed before.

Understanding your customers...

Jane Hardy conducted research into the business networking market before she bought Fabulous Women; she also had some insider knowledge from her role as an Area Leader. However, once she had bought the organisation Jane invested in further research with the existing members. This research looked at:

- What members liked and didn't like about the organisation
- Who they were, including their age group and type and size of business
- Which other networking groups they belonged to or had visited
- Where their businesses were based

In addition Jane commissioned further research into competing organisations and especially their websites.

This research helped Jane to understand where her attention needed to be focused and informed the organisation's marketing plan and a major website update.

Avoiding some common research mistakes

Your friends and family are not good subjects for your research. They are most likely to tell you what you want to hear or, if they are against your idea, their answers will be negative. Even if your friends and family reflect your target market they will not be unbiased customers so their answers will have limited value. However, your friends and family could test out your surveys to make sure that your questions are easy to understand and produce the type of answers you need.

Make sure that you survey enough people in enough different circumstances to establish a valid pattern in the results. If you test your product at a fair on a glorious day and when there is little direct competition for your business the results might be very different to those obtained in a more competitive environment on a more miserable day. You are looking for balance and objectivity.

Do ensure that you are surveying the right people, the people who will be your customers if you go ahead. If you are opening a locally based business you need to survey people who live and work in your area. Don't think you can buy in the results of a survey from a similar business trading in a different place.

A lack of research leads to slower progress...

Many of the business owners contributing to this book own up to too little research at the outset of their businesses. This led to a lack of focused marketing and therefore mixed success in the early days. Their first customers were often a mixed bunch recruited from people they knew or met networking. There was often little to connect purchases. However, by looking for patterns with existing customers the owners featured have begun to redefine their businesses with a clearer, but narrower, service and a more niche target market and have seen their businesses take off.

Their experience suggests that being clear about your offer and target market from the outset will lead to quicker growth but a lack of clarity in the early stages shouldn't stop you from starting. Once you have started, look for the patterns that will lead to greater clarity.

What competition do you have for customers?

Competition comes in many different forms so you will need to look beyond the obvious. If you want to open a new floristry business you will have competition from other local florists, from supermarkets, garages, garden nurseries and other people selling flowers. However, you might have competition from the local chocolate or gift shop as flowers are often bought as gifts. You may find that there is a strong local flower club that offers to arrange flowers for weddings and funerals at a price that you can't match because they don't have your overheads. Look at the research you've done with prospective customers to see what alternative solutions they consider.

When you have identified your competition you need to understand where you can compete.

- What are they good at?
- What are their weaknesses?
- How busy are they?
- What do they charge?
- Who are their target customers?

 What competition does your business face? Competition can be a good thing as it indicates that there is a demand for your product or service. Too much competition can be potentially disastrous. You will need to make it easy for your prospective customers to understand why they should trade with you.

Finding your position in your marketplace

When you do your competitor research you may find some businesses that are struggling to compete. This can be because there are too many businesses competing for the same local market. This doesn't mean that there isn't space to compete just that you shouldn't be competing in the same space as everyone else. One way to identify where there is space for you is to draw up a positioning or perceptual map.

Think about the criteria which customers use to choose one supplier instead of another. You might consider price, quality, convenience, high fashion, classic, designer, mass market or any other differentiating factors. Choose two criteria that are relevant to your business and plot one criterion on the vertical axis and the other on the horizontal axis as illustrated below:

Positioning or Perceptual Map

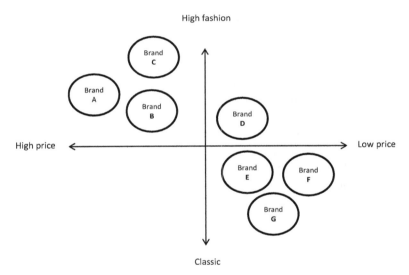

In this illustration we can see that there is significant competition for high fashion items at a high price and for lower priced classic styles. There is potential to compete in lower priced high fashion items but it might be difficult to make a profit in that space. However, there is no competition for classic designs at a higher price so if you can establish that there is a local demand for such designs that would be where you should position your business.

If you can't find space to compete on the first two criteria you choose keep on doing the exercise using different criteria until you find space for your business or until you come to the conclusion that your local market is saturated and you will need to think again.

In summary...

- No business can sell to everyone. You will need to define a clear target market for your product or services
- You will need to understand who will buy, how often and how much they will spend
- You also need to understand what alternative solutions your prospect would consider which will lead you to identify your sources of competition
- Your competition may not be just from similar businesses. You will need to understand your competitors' strengths and weaknesses in order to find your space to compete
- A positioning map can help you to define what your business should be known for

To get you thinking...

- Who will want to pay enough money, often enough for the product or service you want to offer for you to have a viable business?
- How can you set yourself apart from your competitors in a way that will attract your ideal customers?
- Who can help you with the research into your target market and competition?

Action points...

- Think about who you would ideally like to serve
- Research the demand for your product or service
- Research the competition for your business
- Use a positioning map to define where your business will compete

Chapter **7**

Your route to market

'A name indicates what we seek. An address indicates where it is. A route indicates how we get there.'
—Jon Postel

You will need to decide how you will get your product or service to the people who want to buy it. Your decision will be based on what your potential customers want, the resources that you have at your disposal and your personal preference. You may decide that you should have more than one route to market. For example, you may decide to supplement your shop sales with a shopping basket on your website or you may decide to offer outside catering in addition to your café.

Taking on premises

Finding suitable premises on reasonable and affordable terms can be a challenge. Location can be hugely important especially in the retail and hospitality industries. You have to have a very special service and an outstanding reputation if your customers are to go out of their way to trade with you. In retail even being on the wrong side of the road or a short walk can be the difference between success and failure. This is where local knowledge can be very advantageous. Where does your target market seek your type of product or service? Where are the up and coming areas of town? Can you get in early whilst prices are still reasonable and competition may not be so great? Which areas are changing for the worse and should be avoided?

Check with your local authority what developments are being planned. You want to know about housing developments, commercial developments and changes to the road and transport networks. Will these have a positive or negative effect on your proposed business? Talk to other traders in the area to see what their challenges are.

 Consult a lawyer before you sign any contracts. What are you committing to? How easy will it be to terminate a lease early? What are you allowed or obliged to do with the premises? For example can you make the changes you need to offer your services in the way you want to? Will you have to return the premises to the way they were at the end of your lease? What is included in your rent and what arrangements are there for rent reviews? What additional bills will you have to pay, for example business and water rates, repairs etc.?

It's a good idea to check out your landlord too. How easy is it to contact them? Do they keep their promises? How supportive will they be of your business? What short- or long-term plans do they have for the property? You don't want to find yourself signing a lengthy lease with a landlord only to find a few weeks later that they have sold the property to another landlord who has very different plans for the building.

More than one route to market...

Buki Obakin is an accountant so she understands the need for businesses to make money. When she decided to fulfil a long-held dream to open a childrenswear boutique she decided that it made sense to have two routes to market, a bricks and mortar store and an online shop. She investigated vacant properties in a couple of shopping centres, looking at the surrounding businesses, the footfall and the type of people who shopped there. She was able to negotiate a favourable agreement with the leaseholder of a unit in a popular shopping centre due for renovation and so started her bricks and mortar store whilst developing the website as a means to reach a wider audience. She has used social media as a means of driving traffic online and footfall to her store.

Sharing has advantages...

Zoe Angle of Angle Glass designs, makes and repairs stained glass. Many of her projects are very large which makes working from home impossible. However, the costs of renting a studio can be prohibitively expensive. Zoe's solution has been to share a studio with another stained glass artist, which has brought the additional benefits of collaboration for larger projects. In addition both artists have joined with others in their location for some joint marketing through open studio events.

Working from home

Working from home can be a great option for many small businesses but you need to make sure that what you are doing doesn't contravene planning laws. Running your virtual assistant business from a room in your home is unlikely to have an adverse effect on your neighbours but if you are dismantling cars on a shared driveway you will soon find yourself in trouble.

There are tax implications if you run your business from home, especially if you dedicate a part of your premises exclusively for business. So take advice before you make any changes to your property. Will you need planning permission? Will you become liable for business rates on that part of the house? Will you have to pay Capital Gains tax when you come to sell your home? If you rent your accommodation is running a business from home allowable in your lease?

Don't forget to ensure that you have appropriate insurance if you work from home. See chapter 5.

Managing working from home...

Monica Castenetto works from home and ensures a clear demarcation between home and work. This includes a dedicated and organised working space and rules about start and finish times. Monica makes a point of shutting her office door at the end of the working day. She also recommends building in time for getting out and about to avoid the cabin fever effect that many homeworkers describe.

Running a mobile business

Beauty therapy, hairdressing, car and bike repairs, catering, childcare are just some of the businesses that you can run on a mobile basis. This means that you offer your service on your clients' premises, which can reduce your costs and increase your flexibility.

You will need to consider how much chargeable time you will lose for travelling between clients. You may also find that your clients expect to pay a lower fee for a service delivered on their premises. Will the business be financially viable? Are there ways in which you could reduce time spent travelling between appointments, for example by allocating specific times to particular locations?

Flexible solutions

There are an increasing number of flexible options emerging in many areas. For instance, empty shops are being leased on a pop-up basis for short lets. These offer a great way to test the market for your products and to increase your local visibility.

Are there any work hubs that would allow you to rent desk or creative space on a flexible basis? You may be able to rent space by the hour, day, week or longer period. You may just want to book a meeting room on an occasional basis. Many work hubs offer more than just space to their clients. They may offer business support services such as reception or secretarial services. There may be a café or events where you can network with other small business owners and low cost training opportunities.

Online

In the 21st century every business should have an online presence. You only need to look at the shrinking size of the telephone directory to see that prospects are less interested in finding your phone number than searching for you online. Increasingly, customers are doing their research online before visiting your premises or making an appointment.

 What kind of online presence does your business need? Do you need a brochure website, an online store, a Facebook fan page or LinkedIn company page? A website allows you to control what people see and to promote your products and services in the way that you choose. Whilst a social media presence is a good idea if your target market is active on a particular network you cannot control who sees your posts. The social media channels want you to pay for advertising so will limit who can see your free posts.

Would it help your prospects, and you, if your website took bookings? People lead increasingly busy lives and often want to make bookings out of normal business hours so if you can offer them the facility to do this at their own convenience it could increase your business. It is also worth considering whether or not a shopping basket would bring you extra business and open up your offer beyond your immediate locale.

Should you be extending your offer in collaboration with another online business? For example Just Eat and Deliveroo are just two of the companies that are allowing local restaurants to offer home delivery services without the hassle of sorting out the logistics themselves.

In summary...

- How will you get your product or service to your target customers?
- There are advantages and disadvantages in taking on premises or working from home
- Work hubs and pop-up shops may give you more flexibility
- Some types of business lend themselves to a mobile model
- Every business in the 21st century needs an online presence

To get you thinking...

- What impact might your business have on your neighbours and will that affect your choice of location? For example, if you are cooking curry in your kitchen early in the morning will your neighbours complain?
- Are there any planning or insurance implications that might affect your choice of location?
- How does your ideal customer behave online? Which social media platforms are they active on?
- Will collaborating with another business give you an additional lucrative route to market?

Action points...

- Check whether you need premises from which to run your business and work out the cost implications
- Decide which route to market you will use and whether you will launch them all at the same time or plan staggered launch dates
- Start building your social media presence and connections.

Chapter **8**

Developing your brand

'Your brand is what other people say about you when you're not in the room.'

—Jeff Bezos

Don't be tempted to think that a brand and a logo are one and the same thing. Your logo is a part of your brand's identity but your brand is so much more than that. Your brand is what people understand about your business, what they see, hear and feel about you. And it's not just your customers and prospects who are influenced by your brand but also your staff, suppliers and your network.

Branding isn't just something for big corporates either; it is just as relevant to the solopreneur as it is to the global enterprise. A well-conceived brand can be a differentiator between your business and a local competitor so it's worth taking time at the outset to consider how you want people to think about your brand.

Our case studies show that many start-ups don't get to grips with their brands at the outset. This can hamper progress as prospective customers and contacts don't really get what you stand for and why they should buy from you or promote you. Whilst it's perfectly possible to develop your brand as you go, and even to change your brand's visual identity, you can save time by giving it some constructive thought at the outset and that is important when you haven't got time to waste.

What is a brand?

Our purchasing decisions are frequently brand driven. When you buy a new car you probably have a choice of cars that meet your criteria but the chances are that you will be more drawn to one brand than another based on past experience or reputation. When I bought my first car there's no way I would have bought a Skoda because the brand had a reputation for unreliability, which has taken years to shake off. I wouldn't have considered a Volvo either for totally opposite reasons: its reputation for safety made it too middle aged for a 21 year old!

You can probably sum up most well-known brands in one or two words. Take our leading retailers for example; what one or two words would you use to describe each of the following:

- Harrods
- John Lewis
- Harvey Nichols
- Primark
- Marks & Spencer

Whichever words you've chosen you have probably not used the same words to describe two different retailers. That's because the brands have done enough to differentiate themselves in the way you feel about them. The chances are that you don't regularly shop in all of them and your buying behaviour may well have changed over time as you have moved out of one brand's target market and into another.

I wonder if the words that you have chosen are the words that the brand owners would have liked you to choose. For instance, did you use innovation when describing Marks & Spencer? It is one of the company's core values but may not be the first word that people think of when describing the brand. And that's the thing about branding. Branding is how people perceive your business not how you describe it. That doesn't mean you have no influence on your brand but it does mean you can't control it.

How are our perceptions of a brand formed?

The elements that make up a brand are often represented as an iceberg because only a small part of the whole is visible. Those above the 'waterline' include the visual representations of a brand. Things like logo, website, premises and staff uniforms. We choose these to reflect how we want to be perceived by others.

Whilst we may be able to control the elements of branding that people see we have less control over what they feel. Look at some of the negative comments that people post on social media. It used to be said that an unhappy customer would tell five people about their experience and that one in four would tell 20 others. Now people post their views in a Facebook group of 9,000 members or more or give a damning review on TripAdvisor. We can't fully control those things but they do influence the way our brands are perceived.

Developing your brand

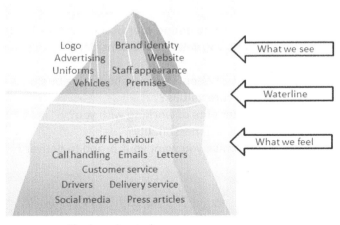

The branding iceberg

Effective brands make sense! Effective brands are those that are consistent in every aspect. When a luxury hotel, charging premium rates, supplies its guests with cheap toilet rolls guests get a negative impression that dilutes the luxury brand. When the driver of a company vehicle drives badly whilst obviously using a mobile phone then the company's reputation is tarnished. When that van is emblazoned with the strapline 'Feel safer with us' the brand is completely undermined (true story!).

Defining what you want your brand to stand for is something that you should do very early in your business' development and certainly before you start designing logos, creating websites or marketing your business. This is important whether you intend to remain a one-person band or to grow your company. It's what will create a professional impression of your business whatever size it is. If you've been working your way through the previous chapters you will be part of the way there. You will:

- Understand your '*why*', your mission
- Have developed your vision for the business
- Have started to think about your values
- Have defined your ideal customer
- Know why your ideal customer will want to buy from you
- Identified your position in the marketplace
- Recognise some of the points of difference between your business and your competitors

All of this will help you to define your brand strategy but there are still more questions you will need to consider:

- What do you want people to feel about your business?
- What are your core values?
- What are the benefits of working with you?
- What's your brand's personality?
- What's the promise you want your brand to deliver?

Pulling your brand together

 It's a good idea to collate your thoughts into one document which can form part of your business plan, help when briefing your designer, form the foundation of your marketing communications and be incorporated into all your policies and procedures. Your document might look like this; there is a copy in your workbook.

Our mission	
Our vision	
Our values	
Our ideal customer is...	
The benefits we can offer our ideal customers are...	
Our ideal customer will choose us rather than a competitor because...	
We'd like people to see our brand as...	
Our tone of voice will be...	

 If you worked your way through chapter 1 you should be able to define your mission and vision. You have probably also defined some personal values but do you want these to be your business' values or do these still need work? Ideally you shouldn't have more than four to six values. Any more become hard to remember. Here are a few ideas to get you started:

Dependable	Visionary	Consistent	Focused
Fun	Learning	Luxury	Inclusive
Honest	Challenging	Nurturing	Dynamic
Integrity	Caring	Clever	Excellent
Reactive	Inspiring	Organised	Courageous
Reliable	Innovating	Value driven	Charitable
Spontaneous	Astute	Efficient	Fair
Supportive	Positive	Different	Easy
Elegant	Curious	Friendly	Approachable
Fit	Conscientious	Confident	Intellectual
Impactful	Insightful	Ethical	Explorative
Professional	Realistic	Resilient	Diverse

The problem with words is that they can mean different things to different people so when you have chosen the words to describe your values it's a good idea to define what they mean to you. For example:

Word	Definition
Stimulating:	we challenge people, including ourselves, to think differently and to try out new things
Supportive:	we support and encourage our clients and each other to grow

Rosanna Henderson's values are fundamental to her mosaic business...

Rosanna doesn't want her art to be seen as elitist so her three core values are:
- *Affordable: start with the client's budget and design work that can be produced for that budget*
- *Quality: whatever the budget the work has to be well made*
- *Client centred: it's really important to Rosanna that the client really likes the commissioned piece so she works closely with her client to understand just what they are looking for, as a result several of Rosanna's clients have become good friends*

Values as a means of differentiation...

Business networking organisation Fabulous Women and Marvellous Men uses its values of collaboration not competition to differentiate itself from most of its competitors. Unlike many of its competitors the organisation does not restrict membership to one person per business category and actively encourages similar businesses to find ways to collaborate as a means of growing their businesses. Fabulous Women and Marvellous Men also collaborates with other networking organisations to provide enhanced opportunities for its members.

In chapter 6 we discussed how to identify your ideal customer, which may have resulted in you defining one or more target audiences. In doing so you should have identified the problem that you will be solving for those customers. The next step is to turn the solution that you provide into a benefit for the customer so that they have a reason to use you. For example, a nutrition coach may offer people who are struggling with their weight a healthy eating programme for which the benefit might be 'so that you can lose weight and sustain the loss with the additional benefit of better health'. A car mechanic may offer a pre-holiday vehicle check 'so that you can be confident your car will cope with the journey'.

Revisit the positioning map and the results of your competitor research to find the reasons why your ideal customer will buy from you rather than a competitor. Finally you should think about your brand's personality and tone of voice. These need to be consistent with other elements of your brand but they can also reflect you as the brand founder.

Take Virgin for example. Although Virgin is a huge brand its personality still shares traits with its founder, Richard Branson. You might use words like edgy, fun, maverick or disruptive to describe the brand's personality. The fact that Branson is more likely to turn up to an interview in jeans and an open-necked shirt rather than the suit and tie favoured by most business executives will not surprise you. Nor would you be surprised to find Sir

Richard riding an elephant to launch a new Virgin Atlantic route to India. All of these things are entirely consistent with the brand.

Finally think about the tone of voice that your brand should adopt to be consistent with your description of the brand. For example, if you've described your brand as fun you don't want to adopt a very formal tone of voice in your communications.

Playing catch up...

Lucy Pitts describes her approach to branding her new business as piecemeal and unimaginative. Strood Copy was named after her house and her branding was a bit nondescript. It was when she heard someone talk about the 'disruptive start-up' at a networking event that the light bulb went on. She realised that the 'disruptive copywriter' fitted her perfectly. It gave her business personality so she briefed a graphic designer to produce a corporate identity that she could really own. Since then her business has taken off. The bright and colourful branding is consistent with Lucy and her approach to life and business and that personality is continued through her speaking engagements and social media interactions.

Evolving over time...

As a life coach, being in touch with her values is a natural process for *Monica Castenetto* but she didn't equate these with her brand until relatively recently. Now Monica realises that her business values are inextricably linked with her own and that people become her coaching clients because of her personal qualities.

> *Her new website reflects this by showcasing Monica's take on life, wisdom and experience and her own brand of life coaching. Her values include integrity, creativity, authenticity, playfulness, rootedness as well as development and learning. She is now actively seeking ways to demonstrate her true personality in her choice of clothing, how she presents herself at events and the way she appears on social media.*

Designing your brand's identity

Now that you are absolutely clear what your brand stands for and how you want it to be perceived you can brief a graphic designer to develop the brand's identity. This might include a logo, typeface, colours, imagery and anything that will convey your brand visually. You might be tempted to try to save money by designing your own corporate identity but, unless you have a background in design or branding, this is usually a mistake. Rebranding is expensive so you want to get it right first time. Be careful with branding that is too 'of the moment' as it could date easily which will not help if you want to be seen as modern and innovative. Working with the right professional should help you to avoid expensive mistakes.

Before you brief a designer check out their work, most will have a portfolio on their website. How original are their designs? Do you like their designs? Is their style compatible with what you are looking for? Ask people whose branding you like if they can recommend their designer.

 Your designer should want to know the answers to the questions in your branding document but will also want to know how you intend to use your branding so think long term not just the immediate future. Think about letterheads, business cards, marketing materials, website, packaging, wrapping materials, PowerPoints, uniforms, shopfronts, vehicles, exhibition stands, handouts, books etc. If there are some logos or corporate identities that you like show them to your designer but make it clear that you are expecting an original design not a clone of someone else's intellectual property.

Your designer should have some understanding of colour psychology and which colours would work best to convey the feel you want for your business but if there are colours you particularly want to use tell your designer at the outset. However, try not to be too inflexible if the colour you want to use doesn't fit well with what you want to achieve.

Once you have chosen your designer you need to agree exactly what you can expect them to deliver:

- How many options will you get for the agreed price?
- How many tweaks will you be able to make before it will cost you more money?
- What happens if you don't like any of the designs?
- Does the fee include designs for stationery such as your business card?
- Are you paying for a logo or a complete branding guide?
- What additional fees might you have to pay e.g. for a specific font?
- How long will it take from brief to first design and then from approval to final artwork?
- Who will own the copyright to the design when you have paid your final bill?

Expect to sign a legal agreement with your designer and to pay a percentage of the agreed fee before any work starts.

Finalising your branding

You may want to get some input from your target market either at the concept stage or before you finalise your options. I remember when I was first developing branding for The Training Pack and was playing with an idea based on a pack of husky dogs the feedback described the design as 'fit for a kennel' and 'suitable for a chocolate box'. I abandoned the idea very quickly. We can get too close to our own ideas and feedback brings in a reality check before we incur too much expense.

Your designer may well supply you with some visuals to show how your branding could be used for the different applications in your brief but if not have a play with it before you make a final decision.

Once you are happy you need your designer to supply you with print-ready, high definition images, including vector versions that will allow you to scale the image for different applications without loss of quality. Make sure that you also have details of the Pantone colours and any fonts used. You don't want to be obliged to go back to your designer every time you want to use your corporate identity. Consider asking your designer to produce a branding guide that becomes your point of reference for your visual identity.

A new look for Bodyline Fitness...

*It was feedback from a couple of clients and the offer of help from a graphic designer client that prompted **Roy Summers** to rethink Bodyline's brand identity. The existing brand had developed over time but was a little bland and did not reflect the growth plans Roy had for the business. He wanted a brand identity that could be applied to all of his marketing, from a new website, to outdoor signage, to sports kit and to promotional items from time to time.*

His designer came up with around 80 concepts, which Roy then whittled down to 10 on which he sought opinions from customers and trainers. Eventually the team settled on a monochrome logo that would work on paper, signage, clothing and more.

Having settled on the design, Roy invested in changing everything over to the new brand identity in a short period. He had new signage made for the outside of the studio, incorporated it into window film for privacy and produced various items of kit for the trainers. Marketing materials were updated and a new website

> *created. The results have had a positive impact on the business and attracted favourable comments from regular clients and prospects.*

Applying your visual branding

Once you have finalised your branding you should use it on everything. Almost certainly you'll need business cards. I recommend printing plenty and carrying them with you all the time (even on holiday). Add your logo to your email signature; apply your branding to your business social media accounts and to your website. It's even worth thinking how you can use it in your clothing when you are attending business events. For example my teal clothing is on brand and makes me stand out in a sea of grey suits so that I've become known for it.

Being consistent in the application of your branding will help make you look professional and that will make you memorable.

Implementing your branding strategy

Of course developing your brand identity is only part of the process of implementing your branding strategy and you will need to take steps to ensure that that strategy runs through everything you do in your business.

Let's start with the above-the-waterline elements, the things that people see. We've mentioned how you dress for business meetings but, if you employ staff, you may want to have a dress code that is appropriate to your brand. Equally, if prospects and customers visit your premises the experience should be consistent with your brand. That might include the decor and organisation, the way they are welcomed and any part of the premises they experience from waiting area or changing room to treatment or meeting room and even the till or checkout process.

Think about your vehicles too, even if they are not branded, if your prospect or customer will see them they will be adding to the impression they gain of your business.

Decide on a house style for your communications. This should reflect your brand's personality and the tone of voice you chose and should be applied to communications of all types from marketing to invoicing, from staff handbooks to your written policies. Your language doesn't need to be stilted just because a document has to be legally binding but it takes skill to achieve something unstuffy but watertight.

It's a good idea to maintain some branding guidelines and share them with your team if you have one. If you outsource things like marketing make sure that you give your supplier access to the guidelines or include the key elements in your brief.

Distinctive within a framework

As network marketers and franchise owners **Gilles and Claire Pelenc** *have little room for manoeuvre when it comes to visual identity however that hasn't stopped them from developing a brand identity of their own.*

Whilst Gilles and Claire benefit from being part of a phenomenally successful worldwide brand it can be difficult to differentiate themselves from other distributors. Gilles and Claire decided that they needed to develop a distinctive brand within a brand and so decided to call themselves the 'Natural Networkers'. They want to be seen as professionals within their fields and people who enjoy an enviable lifestyle, by doing so they aim to attract the right kind of people into their business.

Whilst their personal brand is not represented by a visual identity it is reflected in their social media, offline networking and everyday behaviours. Although it's early days in their new positioning the results so far are very positive.

Staying on brand

It's worth playing the role of customer or prospect every so often and looking at your business through their eyes. Have things crept in that are not 'on brand'? Are your prospects and customers getting the experience you wanted them to have? Think about surveying some of them from time to time and be open to their honest feedback.

Remember that a brand is a perception in other people's minds so be prepared to embrace what people say or to make the changes if what they are saying isn't as complimentary as you would wish.

Whilst you can't control what people think about your business you can influence it. If you manage your customer's experience well they will have no cause to complain. However, mistakes will inevitably occur and it's how you manage them that will make the difference to how people see your business.

Monitor what people are saying about your business online. Check out Facebook, LinkedIn, Twitter and other social media and also sites like TripAdvisor, Trustpilot and other review sites if they are relevant to your business. If you find negative comments apologise for the disappointment but deal directly with the customer to put things right. Don't get defensive and make sure that you avoid a public argument.

If you have staff, use a call-handling centre or outsource other customer-facing aspects of your business. Consider mystery shopping to check that your business is being represented as you would wish.

In summary...

- Branding is about much more than a logo and includes how people feel about your business
- Your branding should be built around your values as well as your 'why', your target market and your offer

- Your brand should have a consistent personality and tone of voice
- Before designing your brand's identity decide all the applications it could be put to
- A branding guide will ensure your identity remains consistent
- Take steps to manage the way people perceive your brand

To get you thinking...

- What do you want people to feel about your business?
- How will your values be reflected in every aspect of your business?
- Where will you be using your brand's visual identity in the foreseeable future? What tangible objects will it be applied to?
- How will you manage your brand's reputation?

Action points...

- Decide what you want your brand to represent
- Complete the designer brief in the workbook before commissioning your corporate identity
- Put together a branding guidelines document and ensure that those producing work for your business (including yourself) refer to it consistently

Chapter **9**

Making a profit

'**Business is all about solving people's problems – at a profit.**'

—Paul Marsden

Whilst your '*why*' may not be fundamentally money driven you will need to make a profit if you are to have a sustainable business. This means that you will have to plan and monitor your finances carefully so in this chapter we'll consider some key financial planning documents, some basic concepts and a moneymaking mindset.

You probably haven't reached your current age without managing a personal or family budget and you may even have run a budget in your earlier career in which case managing your business' finance may hold no fears for you. However, it is the area that seems to cause the most anxiety when I'm teaching start your own business courses, whatever ages the participants, so I will try to keep the chapter as straightforward as possible. My intention is to give you an overview into the subject to allow you to set your prices, complete your business plan and track progress in the first few months of your business. An accountant will be able to produce your year-end accounts, which are a bit more complicated for limited companies than they are for sole traders or, if you want to go it alone, there are numerous books, software packages or courses to help.

Demystifying the jargon

If you're not familiar with business finances you might find the following definitions helpful, other terms will be explained at the relevant points in the chapter:

- *Turnover*: income from sales before any costs are deducted
- *Profit*: profit is what is left when you have deducted all the costs of running your business. Profits are usually split into *gross profit*, which is what you are left with after direct costs have been deducted. *Net profit* is what you are left with when all of the costs associated with the business have been deducted from turnover. The net profit will be what you are taxed on
- *Cash flow*: the progress of money into your business from sales, loans etc. matched with the progress of money out of your business to cover costs etc.
- *Overheads:* costs associated with running the business rather than directly related to sales so things like rent, administration, marketing, utilities. Overheads may also be known as *operating expenses*
- *Break-even*: the point at which your sales income covers the direct costs of sales
- *Assets*: what you or the business owns including cash and payments owed to you
- *Liabilities*: what you or the business owe including outstanding payments you need to make and sales that have been paid for but not yet delivered
- *Balance sheet*: a statement, usually expressed as a table, of your assets and liabilities at a given point in time
- *Budget*: a plan for expenditure usually broken down into key areas and based on estimated income

Establishing your costs

Before you can set prices, work out your start-up finance needs or project your profit potential you will need to consider all of the costs associated with your business. This may seem obvious but it's surprising how often people miss things especially when it comes to paying themselves!

Be realistic with your cost projections. For example, just because you've found some packaging at a bargain price doesn't mean that you'll always be able to buy it at a discount so work on regular prices when you are estimating costs. As a start-up business you may not get the best trade prices until you have established a credit history with the supplier so factor the higher prices in at the planning stage.

 Which costs your business will incur will depend upon the nature of your business but here are some ideas to get you started:

Costs related to sales: make a list of everything that you will need to make the finished product or deliver a specific service and work out the cost of each item. Many people forget to cost in time... time for production, for preparation, for clearing up, for travelling between appointments etc. Be realistic about how much time will be involved and cost it at a sensible hourly rate, that is one that you would be able to hire a suitably qualified person for (even if you will be producing the work yourself you want to earn a reasonable reward for your labours). Don't forget to include packaging where this is necessary to present the product or the incidentals that you need to deliver your service. For example one of my biggest costs is printing.

Premises costs: even if you work from home you'll be spending money on utilities but if you rent premises you may have business rates, maintenance, cleaning and landlord charges etc. Don't forget about insurance and if you work from home do make sure that your insurers will cover your business.

Vehicle and transport costs: remember maintenance, insurance, fuel and parking as well as the cost of purchase.

Equipment: what equipment will you need to buy or lease to be able to run your business? Will you be paying up front or incurring a monthly repayment fee?

Software: this is one of those expenses that easily can be forgotten but if you buy a computer for your business you may also need to buy software for it to be of any use to you. Remember to include things like your cloud-based applications e.g. your accounting software. These days many software packages are sold on a recurring fee basis so keep a note of what is due when.

Professional fees: do you have to pay membership to a trade or professional body to be allowed to practice? Do you require professional indemnity, public or product liability or other specialised insurance? These are all costs that need to be covered. Will you need a lawyer to draw up contracts or agreements? Will you be using an accountant or bookkeeper or other specialist professional?

Marketing: what regular costs will you incur, for instance website hosting or maintenance fees?

Staff costs: will you be paying for regular or ad hoc help that is not directly related to sales and therefore already costed, for example reception or administration?

Make a note of when you expect to have to make payments on the costs you have listed, as this will help you to plan your cash flow.

Setting your prices

There are a number of different strategies that you can use for setting your prices depending upon the nature of your business and your position in the marketplace. There is no right or wrong strategy and you may change yours from time to time but it is important that you approach pricing strategically.

Cost plus pricing

Many businesses work on a basic cost plus a set percentage to work out their prices. This is a rather unsophisticated method that may not lead to a competitive price but at least it ensures that you cover your costs. The percentage you add to your costs will vary significantly depending upon your industry and what your competitors are charging. Do some research to establish what is a typical mark-up in your sector. For instance, if you are selling high fashion that will lose its value at the end of the season you will want to add a higher mark-up to allow you to discount in an end of season sale whilst still covering your costs.

When you've worked out your cost plus price compare it with what your competitors are charging. Is there a significant difference between their price and yours? If so can you work out why? For example are your overheads higher because of your location or are their prices lower because they are part of a big chain with bulk buying power? Be very careful before you slash your prices to compete. You may have to be less ambitious with your profit margins but take care that you don't cut your prices so much that you will be working for little reward. If you do cut your margins can you be sure that you will sell more to make up for the money you will be losing?

Competition pricing

If you are in a very price-sensitive market then you will need to be acutely aware of your competitors' prices and may need to set your prices accordingly. However this strategy can be extremely dangerous if you don't have a very clear understanding of your costs and your profit margins. I have seen a number of businesses fail because they set their prices to undercut the competition without fully understanding all of their costs. It has come as a complete surprise that they have been selling at a loss!

To make this strategy work you will need to keep very tight control of your costs, which may involve you looking at every aspect of your business. Costs can creep up by stealth. Just think about your personal shopping trips, how often do you come home with more than you'd intended to buy? You can't afford to do the same in business if you are operating on very tight margins. If you are the sort of person who doesn't keep on top of your bookkeeping and doesn't monitor expenditure then this is not the right strategy for you.

Value-driven pricing

A better way to compete might be to look at how you can add value to your offer so that you can justify charging a higher price. For instance, many of us pay supermarkets to deliver our shopping to us to save us the trouble of going to the store. Perhaps your customers would value a head massage when they are having a haircut and colour or would welcome a recording of their coaching call with you. You may choose to add a higher-grade component or ingredient to your product to move it into a higher value bracket when compared to your competition. Ideally you want to add something which is low cost to you whilst being of real value or distinctive to your customer.

Penetration pricing

This is not an easy strategy for the small start-up to employ unless you have deep pockets. Penetration pricing depends on slashing prices, sometimes below cost, in order to corner a chunk of the market. It's a strategy that large players will use when moving into a new area and is designed to steal market share from their competitors.

One way in which you could use a version of this strategy would be with a very limited introductory offer in order to get potential customers to try you out. So you charge a loss-leading price for a set number of days or a limited number of customers. To make this strategy work it would need to be accompanied by a strong marketing campaign designed to attract your ideal customer and it needs to be very clear that this is a one-off, time-limited, offer.

At the end of your campaign you would choose a more sustainable pricing strategy.

Skimming pricing

This strategy is best suited to innovative products or the first to the market. Early adopters will usually be willing to pay a premium price to be amongst the first to own the latest innovation. The strategy also works for seasonal products that come to market ahead of competitors, things like new potatoes or home-grown strawberries. Skimming means charging a higher price for a limited period whilst a product is new or only available in limited quantities. Once the product becomes freely available or mainstream the price drops. This strategy can work for small businesses if you can get your product to the market early. Whether this is a temporary or permanent strategy will depend upon what you sell. In the horticultural industry for example you may base your whole business on selling early season, or difficult to obtain out of season, produce that you sell at a premium price. However, if your business is based on being first to market with an innovation you will need to choose an alternative pricing strategy when your product becomes more mainstream.

Don't be tempted to cut your prices because a prospect drives a hard bargain or gives you a hard luck story. These people are often the most difficult to deal with, they want a premium service for a low budget price. If someone doesn't want to pay your asking price discuss which aspects of your offer they are prepared to go without for a reduced price. Make sure that your agreement specifies the agreed price and what you will deliver for it.

Know your worth

A final word on pricing: don't undervalue yourself! Too many of us baulk at charging what we're really worth. We convince ourselves that our target market won't be able to pay a higher rate. The little voice inside our head questions whether we're worth a premium price. We compare ourselves with others and find ourselves wanting. But remember, we only ever see the edited version of another person, what they want us to see, and we are aware of *all* our own foibles and faults so we're not making a straight comparison.

Charging too little may drive away our perfect clients because they will question the quality of our offer as it's too cheap. So make sure that you benchmark your price against your nearest competitors. Don't be tempted to undercut them to gain market share because that is likely to lead to a price war. Instead look for ways to add and communicate your value.

To put this into perspective, if you want to earn £50,000 and you charge £100 per hour you will need to sell 500 hours of your time. But if you only charge £75 an hour you'll have to sell more than 666 hours of time, that's the equivalent of at least four weeks more work for the same money. Let's assume that your average customer pays for five hours of your time at £100. In that case you need 100 customers, but if you charge £75 you'll need more than 133 customers. That means more time and money spent on marketing, on invoicing and on administration so your profits and lifestyle take an even bigger hit. Do you really want to work so much harder for the same money?

You can apply the same principles to products. Let's assume you make high-end jewellery, a necklace takes you three hours to make and the raw materials cost £30. If you sell the necklace for £60 you are paying yourself less than £10 per hour by the time you've factored in utilities and overheads and that's before any selling costs. But will your target customer believe that this is a high-end product made with skill and flair by a specialist jeweller if the cost is just £60? The chances are they will think the item has been mass-produced in a country where wages are low and working conditions poor, or that it is not genuine silver.

The price you charge is one of the factors that positions your product or service in the mind of your ideal customer so as we discussed in the last chapter it needs to be consistent with your brand. When you did your positioning map in chapter 6 you may well have found that the place to compete was in the premium quadrant so don't be afraid to occupy it.

Pricing isn't easy...

Pricing is still a big issue for mosaicist **Rosanna Henderson,** as it is for many artists. She recognised that there is a price cap on what people are prepared to spend at craft fairs and that made it really difficult to make money. Now that she works mainly to commission she has a better formula for working out her prices but it's still difficult to charge for all the time involved.

Nutritionist **Leonie Wright** is another to struggle with pricing and admits that her prices were too low when she started, primarily due to a lack of self-confidence. As her confidence has grown she has been able to increase her prices successfully.

Confidence was also an issue for life coach **Monica Castenetto** when she was setting prices in the early days of her business. Now she takes a more strategic view working out how many clients she can coach well in the time she wants to work, she has redesigned her service to add even more value and set her prices accordingly. Monica describes pricing confidence as something that grows over time.

Copywriter **Lucy Pitts** has found a way to price her services that works for her. She works to an hourly rate and an estimate of the time that each job will take, she then supplies clients with a detailed breakdown of costs and finds that people rarely negotiate.

Planning finance

So now you have an idea of your costs and your prices you can start to complete some of the important financial planning documents. You will need to work out your break-even point as well as budgets and cash flow forecasts. Your budget and your cash flow forecast will be closely related. Your budget will show your planned expenditure for the year whereas your cash flow will project the income and expenditure on a monthly basis.

Budgeting

Setting a budget and sticking to it is an important factor in making a profit – it's all too easy to give in to temptation when there is money in the bank or someone makes you a tempting offer. Having a budget will encourage you to take more considered decisions, for example when you are offered a cut-price deal on advertising or when you are tempted by an early bird inducement.

There are no hard and fast rules about how much you should spend on marketing, much will depend on what you're selling and how competitive your local marketplace is. As a rule of thumb you might like to start with a figure of 5% of your projected turnover but you might want to revise this figure when you've read chapter 11.

Other things you'll want to budget for are accountancy and professional fees, memberships and additional staffing if required. Think about travel expenses or vehicle and equipment maintenance if relevant. It's also a good idea to budget for your personal development and any additional equipment or software that your business may need as it grows.

Producing your cash flow forecast

As we discovered in chapter 3, in business cash is king. If you don't have access to sufficient cash to pay your bills you will be trading illegally, it's therefore vital that you plan and monitor your cash flow carefully. If you are planning to raise finance via traditional routes you may well have to produce three years' of cash flow forecasts. So what is a cash flow forecast?

Basically it's a spreadsheet that records money coming in and out of the business over a chosen period, typically a month, to show how much cash is available at the end of each period. Now that you have worked out your costs and your prices you have much of the information you need to start completing your cash flow forecast.

Projecting income

The next stage is the tricky bit where a crystal ball could help! You now need to estimate how much you will sell each month. Hopefully your market research will have given you an indication of how often people will buy and how much they will spend. However, there is bound to be an element of 'guestimating' for any new business. Do you expect your sales to be seasonal and if so where will the peaks and troughs be? Remember to consider local events and the make-up of your local community when thinking about variations. For example, if you have a big Muslim population your sales may be affected during Ramadan and the dates for that move each year. Are there local festivals that you can take advantage of?

 Do try to be realistic about your projections. How much time does your income figure equate to? How much product will you have to sell and are you confident that you can win that many customers? I remember checking the cash flow forecast produced by a retailer I worked with many years ago which required *every* local resident to spend an average of £5 in her shop every single day! That's never going to happen.

Estimating expenses

Some of your expenses will be easy to predict and plot on to your spreadsheet. For example, regular, known payments such as rent, rates, insurance premiums, loan repayments etc. Others will be predictable in terms of when they go out but you may have to estimate the amount of expenditure involved, for example utilities bills which are not subject to a regular monthly payment.

Other expenses will depend upon sales and these are trickier to predict. Not only do you have to project how much you will sell at what price but also how long the time lag will be between your expenditure and receiving the income.

For instance, if you are making product you will need to buy raw materials before you can make the product, you'll then need time for production before making it available for sale. Will your customer pay cash or will you have to wait for an invoice or credit payment to be made? It can be months between buying the raw materials and receiving payment and that can play havoc with your cash flow. You need to work out realistic predictions for your own business.

Even a service-based business can experience delays between outlay and payment. Suppose you are renting a room in which to see clients, the chances are you will be paying up front for that and only receiving payment from your client when you've delivered the service.

Let's look at an example:

If you are not familiar with cash flow forecasting then we're working with a spreadsheet which shows estimated income and expenditure for a given period, typically month by month for 12 months. The top rows show income and expenses are shown below. At the very bottom of the spreadsheet the total income and total expenditure for the month lead to a balance that becomes the brought-forward figure for the following month. This is the key figure; if it is negative you will need to consider how you can inject sufficient cash to keep trading.

This example shows the cash flow forecast for a massage therapist's first six months of trading. We'll assume that she rents a room that allows her a maximum 32 appointments a month. She charges £45 per session. So if she books 10 appointments in her first month she will generate an income of £450 in that month. Let's assume that her marketing pays off and her business grows steadily each month until she is booking 28 appointments in month six creating an income of £1260 in that month. These figures allow us to plot her income on a month by month basis in sales receipts.

She wants to make sure that her business has enough cash to meet her outgoings in the first few months so she deposits £1000 in her business account. This is the business' only other income in the first six months.

Now we can look at her expenditure. There are two forms of expenditure you will need to plan for, *revenue* is the regular spending on things that have limited life and *capital* expenses are investments in things that will have longer-term value such as equipment, vehicles etc. In this example we're going to keep it simple and concentrate on revenue expenses.

It's easiest to start with known expenses. So we know that the rent is £400 per month, a mobile phone contract is £30 per month, insurance is £20 per month and our therapist is repaying a loan for equipment at £30 per month. Our therapist decides she should do a data protection registration, which is £35 per year and she pays this in month one. She also has membership of her professional body to pay for and this is due in month four. These are all plotted on to the appropriate rows.

Now we need to plot the variable expenses such as marketing. Our therapist prints some leaflets and business cards and joins a networking group that gives her upfront costs of £300. She's going to do a direct mail campaign in month two and month five and will attend a couple of networking events every month. These account for the monthly fluctuations in marketing expenses.

Now that she can see her monthly balances she can work out how much she can afford to pay herself each month so can plot that figure as a salary. Of course this might be the first figure that you put into your forecast, especially if you are the main breadwinner and need to earn a minimum amount to meet your obligations.

 This example is a very straightforward one; there are more complex versions and a template for you to do your own in the workbook.

Cash flow forecast

Month	1	2	3	4	5	6
INCOME						
Sales receipts	£ 450.00	£ 720.00	£ 900.00	£ 1,080.00	£ 1,170.00	£ 1,260.00
Cash introduced	£1,000.00					
INCOME TOTAL	**£1,450.00**	**£ 720.00**	**£ 900.00**	**£1,080.00**	**£ 1,170.00**	**£ 1,260.00**
REVENUE EXPENDITURE						
Salary	£ -	£ 400.00	£ 600.00	£ 600.00	£ 800.00	£ 800.00
Rent	£400	£400	£ 400.00	£ 400.00	£ 400.00	£ 400.00
Telephone	£ 30.00	£ 30.00	£ 30.00	£ 30.00	£ 30.00	£ 30.00
Marketing	£ 300.00	£ 50.00	£ 20.00	£ 20.00	£ 50.00	£ 20.00
Memberships				£ 150.00		
Data protection	£ 35.00					
Insurance	£ 20.00	£ 20.00	£ 20.00	£ 20.00	£ 20.00	£ 20.00
Loan repayments	£ 30.00	£ 30.00	£ 30.00	£ 30.00	£ 30.00	£ 30.00
TOTAL REVENUE	**£ 415.00**	**£ 530.00**	**£ 1,100.00**	**£ 1,250.00**	**£ 1,330.00**	**£ 1,300.00**
BALANCE B/F		£ 1,035.00	£ 1,225.00	£ 1,025.00	£ 855.00	£ 695.00
INCOME	£ 1,450.00	£ 720.00	£ 900.00	£ 1,080.00	£ 1,170.00	£ 1,260.00
EXPENSES	£ 415.00	£ 530.00	£ 1,100.00	£ 1,250.00	£ 1,330.00	£ 1,300.00
BALANCE	**£1,035.00**	**£ 1,225.00**	**£ 1,025.00**	**£ 855.00**	**£ 695.00**	**£ 655.00**

It's probably a good idea to do more than one version of your cash flow forecast to make sure that your business will still work if some of the variables change. For instance what will happen if your business grows faster than expected? This might seem like something that you should relish but it can be catastrophic if you don't have the cash available to support the faster growth.

Imagine you win a contract to supply a major retailer with your organic skincare range. They decide that they want to stock the range in 25 stores and they need a minimum delivery of two dozen of each of three product lines for each store. Wow! What a fantastic order, 156 dozen items in one sale. But wait a minute... you need 1872 jars to package your skincare in, you need the raw ingredients to make the range and now you need some extra help with production... suddenly your costs have rocketed. These are expenses that your business will have to fund for several months because the supermarket isn't going to pay you before they've taken delivery and may make you wait a further 60 to 90 days before making the payment. Can you afford to carry that amount of debt?

It's not all bad news because a signed contract from a major supermarket may be enough to persuade the bank to lend you money or give you an overdraft so cash flow may not be a problem. However, whichever way you borrow money you will have to pay interest so your costs have gone up. But the supermarket will probably have driven a hard bargain because their profit margins are very tight so have you actually agreed a price that will allow you to make a profit?

Cash is king...

Cash is king! If you run low on cash, you'll spend a huge proportion of your time firefighting and not actually working on the business. **Giles Button** *dedicated every Friday morning to accounts, checking where the business was and also keeping on top of money owed. It's very important to be professional with customers and get them into a routine of paying within a fair timescale.*

Dealing with cash flow problems

Even profitable, successful businesses can have problems with cash flow, which is why it is vital to track it in your business. Problems can occur when your business grows more rapidly than planned, when customers pay more slowly or costs are higher than forecast. You will need to be really clear about why you have problems with cash flow. For example have you taken your eye off the ball with expenses or invoicing or were you undercapitalised at the start? Were your sales estimates too ambitious or did you get the correlation between expenditure and income wrong? When you understand the nature of the problem you can take action to overcome it. You could:

- Inject more cash into the business from your own resources or via a loan or overdraft
- Take deposits up front or shorten your payment terms
- Offer a discount for prompt payment
- Set up a trade account to pay your suppliers rather than paying cash on delivery
- Increase your prices
- Cut your costs
- Factor your invoices: you sell your invoice to a factoring company or bank which will take a percentage for collecting the money on your behalf but will give you the cash up front. This means that you will get less money overall but will get cash promptly. However, not all invoices will be accepted by the factoring organisation.

Working out your break-even point

One of your most important financial projections will be the calculation of your break-even point. This is the point at which your costs are covered and you can look forward to making some money!

In order to work out your break-even point you need to understand the difference between fixed and variable costs.

Fixed costs are those expenses that a business is committed to whether or not it sells anything. They include rent, rates, loan repayments, insurance and salary costs. **Variable costs** are those that are directly related to generating sales and fluctuate according to how much you sell. They will include raw materials, packaging, delivery and additional staffing costs.

Here's a simple way to calculate your break-even point. First you need to work out your fixed costs for a given period, this can be a day, a week or a month. In this example we'll use a month:

Salary	£ 2000
Rent	£ 400
Insurance	£ 50
Loan repayments	£ 100
Total	**£ 2550**

Now assume you are making widgets. The costs per widget are:

Raw materials	£ 25
Packaging	£ 1
Delivery	£ 5
Total	**£ 31**

Research tells you that you should be selling your widgets for £80 each.

The difference between the selling price and the cost price is £49. This needs to help pay for your fixed costs so the difference between the direct costs and the selling price is known as the *contribution.* By dividing the fixed costs by the contribution you can work out how many widgets you need to sell in order to break-even. In this case the fixed costs of £2550 are divided by the contribution of £49 so you need to sell 53 to cover your direct and fixed costs. Sell more than 53 and you make a profit, sell less and you'll make a loss.

However, this calculation doesn't include overheads such as marketing and administration so in reality you will need to sell more than 53 widgets to run your business and still make a profit.

Raising finance

 By now you should have some idea how much finance you will need to start your business and to keep it going for a few months until you get beyond your break-even point.

Do you have access to sufficient cash yourself or will you need to raise some finance? If so there are a number of options you can consider. You need to remember that investors will make their decision based on your business plan and also on you. If you watch programmes like Dragons' Den you will quickly realise that the person behind the business is almost more important to investment decisions than the business itself. You'll need to understand your business plan inside out and be particularly clear about the numbers and how you will make money. Investors will be looking for a business that is scalable so it will need to be able to make money in ways that don't depend just upon you selling your time on a one to one basis.

These are your options:

Bank loans

There was a time when this was the primary route to start-up finance but banking industry crises have made banks more and more reluctant to fund start-ups. However, as a more mature entrepreneur you may well have a good track record with your bank, as well as assets which can be used to secure a loan, so it is worth having a conversation with your bank to see what help they can give. You will need to consider how much of your hard earned property you are prepared to risk and will need to have the agreement of your partner and family if you are risking shared assets. You can't reasonably expect a lender to risk their capital if you are not prepared to take some risk yourself. You will need a business plan, but most banks have free templates that will allow you to produce the information they need. Your completed workbook should give you all the information you need to complete a formal business plan.

If you are turned down for a bank loan it is worth investigating government-backed loan guarantee schemes to see if you are eligible.

Crowdfunding

This is a relatively recent method of raising finance and allows you to pitch your idea to a wider public via the internet. There are numerous platforms to choose from depending on what you are trying to achieve. The big difference between crowdfunding and traditional methods is that crowdfunding allows a lot of people to back you with a little money whereas the traditional routes look for large sums from few backers.

Of course if people are going to back your business there will need to be a benefit to them. One route allows you to sell shares in your business, which means that your shareholders will benefit from a share of the profits in your business whilst taking the risk that there will be some. Another is to raise capital in exchange for a reward which might be a product sold at an advantageous price, a PR opportunity for a backer's business or admission to an exclusive event.

Don't make the mistake of thinking that crowdfunding is the easy option. It takes a great deal of effort and marketing activity to make it work. When it does work the results can be spectacular but many businesses fail to reach their targets and then get none of the money they have pitched for. Try to be creative to help your pitch gain traction. One exponent of the art is Ginger Wildheart who has used the medium to raise funds for his albums, and a book, and consistently exceeded his target many times over. Search for 'Ginger Wildheart Pledge Video' on YouTube for one of the pitches he made which helped a campaign raise 555% of its target, a word of warning though... the language is not very businesslike but it spoke to his audience.

For more information about crowdfunding and some of the UK's platforms visit http://www.ukcfa.org.uk/ but remember that you could look at international crowdfunding sites too.

Venture capitalists and business angels

This option might appeal to you if you have ambitions to grow a big business but will probably be less appealing if your vision is a small, locally based business with you at the helm. Venture capitalists and business angels have money and are prepared to take risks with that money to back businesses with high growth potential. Typically they buy shares in the company and they look to sell them at a profit after five to eight years.

As with all forms of finance there are advantages and disadvantages. Because the investment is high risk your backer is likely to drive a hard bargain and take a bigger share of your business than you might like. However, you will have access to the business or individual's business experience and contacts, which can be invaluable.

If you feel this is an option you want to consider then do your homework. Choose someone with the right experience, contacts and personality to enhance your business. A business angel might be more willing to invest time and expertise in your business than a venture capitalist who is more focused on investing money to make money.

Friends and family

Borrowing from those who know and love you is another very traditional way for start-ups to raise finance but it can be fraught with difficulty. Make sure that you are absolutely clear about the risks involved and when you expect to be in a position to start repaying the money. Draw up a proper agreement that includes interest payable and terms and make sure you honour it. You don't want your new business to destroy the relationships that are important to you.

Taxation

I always remember moaning about having to pay tax when I first started work and my Dad telling me that at the same age his one big ambition was to earn enough to pay tax. I think that's a great philosophy. If your business makes money you will need to pay tax and you'll need to make sure that you have access to the cash to pay your tax bills when they are due.

In the UK tax is collected by Her Majesty's Revenue and Customs (HMRC) and they have lots of information and webinars to help owners of small businesses get taxation right. The main areas of taxation that most small business owners will need to think about are:

- Income tax: this is payable by both sole traders and company directors. Directors will probably pay via payroll with regular deductions. Sole traders will need to file a self-assessment form and pay tax twice yearly on 31st January and 31st July. Normally sole traders pay 'tax on account' for the following year and these figures are based on your previous year's earnings with any adjustment being made on 31st January. However, in your first year there will be no history upon which to base the payment on accounts so you may well find yourself paying tax for at least 18 months in your first payment. If you don't plan for this it can be a real issue for your cash flow. There are heavy penalties if you don't file your return on time (the tax office will tell you when it is due) and if you don't pay what you owe by the deadline.
- Corporation tax: this is paid on the profits of companies. You will need to prepare full accounts and complete a Company Tax Return. Using an accountant may well save you money.
- VAT (Value Added Tax): you will need to register for VAT if your turnover hits the VAT threshold in any period of 12 months (check the HMRC website for details.) Most goods are subject to VAT but there is a list of items such as many foods that are not liable to VAT. Once you have registered

for VAT you will need to charge VAT on your sales but will be able to reclaim the VAT you pay on eligible purchases. There are various schemes in place for small businesses so I recommend consulting an accountant for advice on the best option for your business. You can register for VAT voluntarily below the threshold but think about the implications on your prices... if your customer is not able to reclaim the VAT you have just put up your prices by the current rate of VAT.

Registering for VAT can have its advantages...

Giles Button says, 'I'd definitely advocate registering for VAT, so that you can claim back VAT. This was a "no brainer" for me, as we worked in B2B (Business to Business) so almost all clients could claim back the VAT we charged and it also gave more credibility to the business when it was young.'

Remember that your business income represents one aspect of your finances. You may have other sources of income such as a pension, interest and dividends, which will all need to be reported in your tax returns.

Tracking progress

Forecasting your finances is a key part of business planning but once you start trading you need to track your progress on a regular basis. The tighter your financial position the more frequently you will need to review your figures. Here are some of the questions you need to answer:

- How do sales compare to forecast: think volume, value and timing?

- How do expenses compare to forecast: is the relationship between sales and expenditure what you expected it to be?
- How long are customers taking to pay their invoices and is there anything you can do to speed this up?
- Is growth happening as planned or do you need to adjust the forecasts to take account of higher or lower growth rates?
- Is there sufficient cash available to the business to meet current and foreseen liabilities?
- Do you need to spend more to boost business e.g. on marketing or in sales?
- Is the business making a profit?

Some winning tips from business owners...

Although **Lucy Pitts** didn't have much of a plan when she started her business she has developed one as her business has taken off. She now has daily targets for what she wants to earn and, despite doubling them, has never missed one. She has identified nine possible income streams and is in the process of prioritising them.

Giles Button recommends staying on top of the numbers: 'I'd always done basic bookkeeping in house but learned that it was better to pay someone to come in. Knowing the numbers was crucial to check that we weren't just building turnover, but were actually making a profit.'

In summary...

- Every business needs to make a profit. Understanding costs and setting the right prices is vital
- One of your first tasks will be to estimate all of your costs remembering to factor in time for all the different activities that you will need to perform
- There are a number of different ways to set your prices but having the confidence to charge enough money from the outset is important
- Setting and maintaining a budget will help you to control expenditure and ultimately to make a profit
- A cash flow forecast will predict potential problems and plan to mitigate them. Monitoring cash flow will be vital if you are going to trade legally
- Understanding your break-even point will help with some decision making
- Consider your options for raising any necessary finance based on your longer-term ambitions for the business and the degree of control you want over it
- You will need to understand what taxation you are liable for from the outset and factor this into your financial plans
- Tracking your financial progress should be a routine task especially if you are operating on tight margins

To get you thinking...

- How much start-up finance will you need? What expenditure is vital and what is desirable?
- How much do you need to earn each month?
- How will you set your prices?

Action points...

- Work out a survival budget so that you know the minimum you need to earn each month to be able to live.
- Work out your start-up and routine costs
- Complete your cash flow forecasts, budget and break-even analysis
- Investigate your options for raising finance if needed and the process that you will need to follow to apply for finance, including timescales
- Register with the tax authorities when you start trading. Decide whether or not to register for VAT

Chapter **10**

Putting your customer at the heart of your business

> The golden rule for every businessman is this: 'Put yourself in your customer's place.'
>
> **—Orison Swett Marden**

There is a danger that we design our businesses around the lifestyle we want to lead, this can be particularly true for the more mature entrepreneur. We want to escape a corporate straightjacket, create a work-life balance around our families or our retirement and we want to live our *why*. The problem with designing our businesses around ourselves is that this may not be the best fit for our ideal customers, which will make it hard for our businesses to take off. We need to keep the customer at the centre of our business and then find ways to make that work for us. In this chapter we're going to look at how we can do this.

If you have done some effective research you will know how your ideal customer wants to access your products or services and you will understand what they are unhappy with from their current solution. The results will help you to design your business around your ideal customer and, if you've done your competitor research, should help you establish a point of difference. So how do you design your business around your ideal customer?

Mapping the customer journey

It's time to get inside your ideal customer's shoes and think about their journey to and through your business. This exercise will allow you to apply what is known as the marketing mix to your business. The marketing mix refers to:

- Product
- Place
- Price
- Promotion

And in its extended version includes:

- Physical evidence
- People
- Process

We've already started to think about some of these things but by mapping the customer's journey through your business we will test whether your plans are right and whether there are any gaps in the plan that still need to be plugged. This process will take time but is fundamental to setting up your business for success.

So what are the key points in your customer's journey? Typically they are:

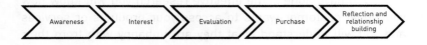

So you need to think about what your customer wants to know and experience at each of these points. Some of the answers will come directly from your business but there will be others that you have less control over, as we considered in looking at your brand and the influences below the waterline. There will be some points at which the answer or experience will be critical to the prospect's next move; these are often called 'moments of truth'. For example, if your prospect wants to book an appointment with you but nobody picks up the phone she may well go to your competitor who answers swiftly.

So let's start the journey...

Nobody can buy from a business they've never heard of so the first thing you will need to think about is how prospects are going to find out about you. Before you start thinking about promotional activities you need to understand what your customer does and doesn't know. For example, do they know that the service you offer exists and is what they are looking for or do they just recognise that they have a problem but don't know what the solution is?

Let's imagine that your ideal customer is a 40-year-old woman who is stressed and overwhelmed juggling a family, career, home and social life. She's reached breaking point, she can't sleep, she's got a constant headache, she's snapping at everyone, she's either not eating or overeating and she may be drinking too much. She probably understands she has a problem but does she label it as stress? Perhaps she just thinks she needs some migraine relief or sleeping pills from the doctor. She may not be aware that acupuncture, massage therapy, coaching, yoga and mindfulness are just some of the alternative solutions for dealing with her problem. Or perhaps it's your cleaning, ironing or childcare service that could help her.

 So some of the questions you need to think about as you map the first stage in your customer's journey are:

- What's the problem or problems I solve for my customers?
- How does my ideal customer define their problem?
- Does my ideal customer understand that what I do is a solution to their problem?
- Is my product or service likely to be the first solution they think of?
- How and where will my ideal customer look for a solution to their problem?
- What will they search for? How will they type that search into Google?

As you answer these questions you may wish to refer back to the work you did on defining your ideal customer in chapter 6.

The next step is to think of all the different ways in which you could raise awareness of your product or service. At this stage don't be judgmental; list as many as you can think of, you can decide which would be most appropriate later. Here are some ideas to get you started:

- Website
- Social media
- Press/media articles
- Networking
- Listing sites/directories
- Advertising
- Signage on premises or vehicles
- Shopfront
- Joint ventures
- Sponsorship
- Referrals

Once you have a list of options you can start to think which would be right for your business. This is where we go back to your prospect and their understanding of the possible solutions to their problem. If our lady knows that she wants to hire a cleaner then she may well look in a local directory or search for a cleaner online. However, if she's unaware of the solution she may type her symptoms or her problem into an internet search. This means that you will need an online presence where you have described the problem in words similar to hers and then offered your solution. Or perhaps you will need to attend networking events where you have an opportunity to talk about the problems you solve and how your service helps. We'll explore how you get your message across in the next chapter.

The workbook will help you to decide how you will raise awareness in your business.

Having gained awareness you will need to develop your prospect's interest. The aim is to help your prospect understand what you do and how you can solve their problem. This really means engaging with the internal conversation your prospect is having. Let's go back to our stressed-out mum. She's probably saying something like, 'I wish I could get rid of this headache. If only I could sleep better I'd feel better and if I didn't have so much to do...' You get the picture.

What is the internal talk that your ideal customer is having? What is their pain? How does the pain make them feel? What are their symptoms? What is the pain stopping them from doing? How is the pain affecting their relationships or ambitions? How would removing the pain make them feel? Write down the answers because they will help you to craft your marketing message, which we'll consider in the next chapter. They will also help you to think about the vehicles you can use to get the message out.

So if a Google search got your ideal customer to your website the words on the page need to speak to her. If she heard your introduction at a networking meeting the next step would be a one to one. Think now about the different ways that you could move the person who has just heard of you to the next step where they are interested in what you do. This is one of your moments of truth; if you don't capture her interest here you may well have lost her. Here are some ideas:

- A brochure
- Website
- Blog
- Talks
- Video
- Shop window/product display
- Newsletter
- Customer referrals
- Promotional offers

You have probably seen by now that there isn't a hard dividing line between generating awareness and creating interest, the two should follow naturally and then lead on to the next step.

Try before you buy...

Egidija Bailie *hand makes a range of cosmetics, which she retails under her brand, EE's Cosmetics. In addition to her website Egidija raises awareness through extensive networking where she generates interest by offering samples for people to try. She also works collaboratively with other business owners to spread the word. For example, Travel Counsellor Cathie O'Dea includes a small selection of tester pots, suitable for travellers, as a gift when she sends clients their travel packs; the pots are accompanied by a marketing postcard.*

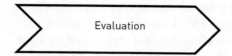

Evaluation

So now that you have your prospect's interest you need to move them towards buying but for many businesses there will be a step in between where they compare you with the alternative solutions. Start by thinking about the factors they will compare, these will vary according to the type of business you are running and the size of the customer's investment, but will probably include some of the following issues and maybe others:

- Location: how convenient is it? How easy is it to get to? Is it accessible by public transport? Can they park and how much will that cost?
- Opening hours: are you open when they want to use you?
- Appointments/bookings: how easy is it to make an appointment? Can they access your booking system 24/7 or do they have to speak to you?
- Results: what results can they expect from working with you?
- Credibility: do they believe that you have the skills, qualifications, experience, time, resilience to deliver for them?
- Quality: are your products and services of the quality that they expect? Is the quality consistent with the price?
- Environment: will they feel safe and comfortable? Does the environment make them feel welcome, valued and respected?
- Price: what's included in the price? Is the price fixed or an estimate?
- Value: are you offering good value for money?
- Chemistry: does your prospect like and trust you? Can you work together?
- Product/service: how well does your product or service fit their needs?
- Delivery: how flexible are the options? How easy is it for them to get your product or service at a time that they need or want it?

At this point in the journey your prospect is seriously considering buying from you so you need to help them towards a decision by making the purchase as risk free as possible. Look at your answers to the above questions and think how you can provide reassurance or the chance to try you out. Which factors are critical to their decision making?

Which of these ideas would be relevant for your business?

- Product samples
- Demonstrations
- Discovery calls
- Trial sessions
- Home visits
- Money-back guarantees
- Fitting rooms
- Job specifications and quotations/estimates
- Test 'drives'
- Testimonials
- Case studies with results
- Before and after pictures

The customer journey in practice...

Maureen Bailey *owns VA Curtains; she is a highly talented and well-qualified soft furnishings expert. Her primary sources of raising **awareness** are her website and Facebook, networking and customer referrals.*

*She generates **interest** through one-minute pitches at networking events, displaying sample products, a newsletter, her website and customer testimonials. Her Facebook page shows photos that demonstrate her attention to detail as well* as the finished product in situ. Maureen's message goes beyond the obvious of making your home look good to saving money by keeping out draughts with interlinings, getting a better night's sleep and getting the kids to sleep on light evenings with blackout linings.

Once Maureen has an enquiry she will make a home visit taking samples of her work and pattern books with her. She takes measurements, gets a feel for the prospect's taste and demonstrates her abilities with the samples and client testimonials. She helps the prospect to choose a suitable fabric and then produces a detailed quotation that takes into account design details, fitting, delivery time etc. This allows the prospect to **evaluate** Maureen's offer against alternatives in order to reach a decision. It also allows Maureen's prospects to get to know, like and trust her which helps to secure the sale.

Purchase

So you've cleared all the hurdles and your prospect is now ready to buy. Fantastic! However, before you take the money there are a few other things you need to consider. You'll need to think about the buying process as well as the experience that your customer receives. I'm not suggesting that you wait to make a sale before considering these things; they should all be part of the plan, which starts with your customer at its centre. Some of these points will be critical to your customer's experience and their willingness to trade with you again and to recommend you.

Let's start with the process.

- How will you collect and store vital information e.g. customer contact details?
- Does your customer need to sign a contract or agreement? If so how will you make sure that they understand what they are signing for and what protections are in place for you and them?
- Do you need a deposit? If so how much, how does it need to be paid and under what circumstances would it be repaid or forfeited?
- When are further payments or the balance due and how will they be collected? How will you invoice to ensure prompt payment?
- What payment options does your customer have? E.g. cash, credit, BACS transfer etc.
- If there are optional elements to the service how do you ensure that the customer's choices are recorded and communicated to those who need to know?
- How do you allocate the time and resources required to fulfil the customer's contract? For example, if a customer has booked your vintage car for her wedding how will you ensure that it can't be double booked? How do you ensure that your colour specialist has the time to finish one client's hair before starting the next?
- What's the process for confirming bookings, venues, phone calls etc.? Will you have a reminder system to avoid no-shows?
- How will you pack items to ensure safe delivery? Will you use a courier or post? How will you insure against loss or damage? How will you deal with non-delivery or breakages?

This list is not comprehensive but should form the basis for you to think through the processes that you need in your business when the customer makes the decision to buy.

Now we need to think about the customer experience and all the touch points that can influence their satisfaction. How did you rate the restaurant the last time you went out for a meal? What factors influenced that rating? I'll bet it was more than just the food. Compare your list with mine:

- How easy was it to book?
- Did the restaurant check if we had any special needs either for food or access?
- Confirmation or reminder of booking
- Greeting on arrival
- Was my coat and umbrella taken from me and put somewhere safe?
- Was our table ready?
- Were we offered a drink?
- Was the table nicely laid?
- Were the flowers fresh and bug free?
- Was the menu well presented and with plenty to tempt me?
- Was the waiter well informed about the menu and the ingredients?
- Were the wine options interesting, affordable and well matched with the food?
- How long did we have to wait for each course?
- Was the food at the appropriate temperature and attractively served?
- Did the food match the menu description and did I enjoy it?
- How did I feel about the music or lack of it?
- How was the ambiance?
- How comfortable were the chairs?
- Were the toilets clean, pleasant and adequately equipped?
- Did anyone check that all was well with my meal or that I had everything I needed?
- How was my bill presented?
- How easy was it to pay by my chosen method?
- Was my coat and umbrella returned to me in a timely manner?
- Was I thanked for my business?

You may have had more on your list and you may have included factors like how good the company was or the impact that other guests had on your experience.

 So now think about your customer, what are all the touch points in your service delivery? How can you ensure that they all work smoothly and contribute to a value for money customer experience that is in line with your brand and position in the marketplace?

Which of these factors can you control? How can you influence the factors over which you don't have direct control? For example, do you need to set clear expectations for your suppliers? Do you need to do some checks prior to service delivery such as checking out the room you've booked for a meeting, sampling the menu or monitoring the cleanliness of the toilets? Do you need to train your staff or representatives?

When you understand how your customer will judge you you can put systems and processes in place to ensure that they will have a great experience. You may want to look at your list and decide which factors are critical to a good experience, your moments of truth, and which may have less influence. For example, the quality of food would be critical for most restaurants.

An outstanding example...

A few years ago we booked a few days at Residence Agnes in Prague. A couple of days before we travelled I received an email from the hotel's manager asking what they could do to make our stay a good one. We had read that taxi drivers in Prague tended to charge tourists over the top prices so we asked if the hotel could arrange a cab from the station for us. Not only did they arrange the cab but also told us how much the fare should be. Our first step in the customer journey was excellent and the rest of our experience at the hotel matched it.

> Reflection and
> relationship building

Your customer's journey doesn't stop with the service delivery. If you are going to build a sustainable business you will need to find a way to gain repeat sales or recommendations from your existing customers. This should be part of your planning process and not left to chance.

It's worth noting that for every customer who complains there are possibly 25 more that say nothing but take their business elsewhere. They may not be telling you about their negative experience but they may well be posting it on social media or a feedback site like TripAdvisor. Bill Gates describes unhappy customers as a business' greatest source of learning so you need to hear from them. Make it easy for people to complain to you and make sure your customers know how to do it.

 Consider how you will gather customer feedback. Some people include a feedback form with an invoice, others will issue an evaluation form at the end of an event and others will employ a third party to call a number of customers for their views. Keep your process as simple as possible. Many businesses will simply ask their customers how likely they would be to recommend them to others on a scale of one to ten. Ideally you would want to capture contact details so that you could follow up with those who wouldn't recommend you. Find out why and try to put the matter right. Customer loyalty is frequently acquired by solving a problem to a customer's satisfaction.

Don't just follow up the unhappy customers but get in touch with those who rated you at nine or ten, thank them and ask them why they gave you that score. Ask if you can quote them and add them to your testimonial bank (N.B. it's important to collect testimonials from the word go).

Hopefully your happy customers will be good for repeat business but even they will forget about you if you don't stay in touch so consider how you will develop an ongoing relationship with your customers. Would they be interested in a newsletter? Could you hold 'by invitation only' customer events? Should you be sending thank you letters? I once received a thank you letter from the director of a company from whom I'd bought an inexpensive hat stand in the sale. But don't stop there; find ways to follow up further to maintain the relationship. So if you are a weight-loss coach you might write to congratulate a client on reaching their goal weight. You might then give them a call in a couple of months' time to see if they've maintained their new weight and to offer tips for getting back on track if not. You might follow up a few months later and if your client is still succeeding you might ask them if they would be willing to be a case study. Perhaps you could send them a small reward for success such as a bunch of flowers.

Ask your happy customers for testimonials and referrals. There's a tendency to view the sort of testimonial that says, "'the service was excellent" GS London' as made up by the business so ask for full names, videos or post copies of letters (with the customer's permission, especially if contact details are visible). It's worth thinking about a system for encouraging referrals, perhaps a time-limited discount for the existing customer to pass on to their contact with a similar reward for the customer to use against their next purchase. Alternatively, a bouquet of flowers or a voucher will always go down well. Even a thank you card or call will be appreciated.

An extract of a customer journey map for Fabulous Women and Marvellous Men

	Awareness
'Customer' viewpoint	Never heard of you!
Marketing and sales activity and information	• Website • Facebook page • Twitter • Posters • Expos • PR and advertising • Marketing material • Members invite guests • Group Leaders mailing their own lists • Listing sites and networking directories
Process to be completed	• Website to be kept up to date and functioning • Facebook page to be regularly updated including details of meetings
Touch points/ Moments of truth	• Visitors to website must be able to find required information easily
Who is involved and what are they responsible for?	• Marketing department for producing and updating materials • Webmaster: ensuring functioning website

	Interest
'Customer' viewpoint	I might want what you offer but do I want it from you?
Marketing and sales activity and information	• Website download • Facebook page • Twitter • Expos • Direct mail • Social evenings open to non-members
Process to be completed	• Visitors can book to attend meetings via the website or can get further information via phone or email • Autoresponders to request for free download
Touch points/ Moments of truth	• Ease of booking on website • Download must arrive in subscriber's inbox promptly
Who is involved and what are they responsible for?	• Marketing department for producing and updating materials • Webmaster: ensuring functioning website

	Evaluation
'Customer' viewpoint	You're on the shortlist so prove that you can deliver what I want/need
Marketing and sales activity and information	• Guests welcome to attend up to three meetings without joining • Welcome email from Group Leader • Visitor months allow former members and guests who've previously attended three meetings to take another look
Process to be completed	• Visitors book via website or direct with Group Leader • Head Office tracks visitor attendance
Touch points/ Moments of truth	• Welcome and experience at the meeting
Who is involved and what are they responsible for?	• Group Leader (Area Leader if present) welcoming guest and introducing to members • Members making guests welcome

	Purchase
'Customer' viewpoint	You've got my money now earn it
Marketing and sales activity and information	• Welcome letter and thank you card from owner Jane Hardy • Membership handbook • Invitation to join one or more member exclusive Facebook groups
Process to be completed	• Welcome letters including website login, membership badge etc. • Payment processed
Touch points/ Moments of truth	• Warmth and speed of welcome
Who is involved and what are they responsible for?	• Admin for on-boarding • MD for personalised welcome • Group Leader recruiting new members

	Reflection and relationship building
'Customer' viewpoint	Either that was great how do I get more of it or That was disappointing (or worse) and I'm going to tell everyone to avoid you!
Marketing and sales activity and information	• Direct contact with owner Jane Hardy • Promotion via social media and newsletters according to membership level • Birthday cards • Opportunities to share achievements and more via FWMM's social media • Additional services according to membership level
Process to be completed	• Regular Facebook invitations to share information • CRM updates
Touch points/ Moments of truth	• Members receiving what they have paid for • Pleasant surprises
Who is involved and what are they responsible for?	• Admin for keeping member records updated • Group Leaders for looking after members • MD for personal attention

 Your workbook contains a template for you to develop your own customer journey map.

Making the journey work for you

So now that you are aware of all the activities that make up the customer journey you can start to think about how that works for you and identify where you might need help if you are to live your ideal lifestyle. We'll consider this in chapter 12.

In summary...

- Mapping your customer's journey will allow you to structure your business to make your customers happy
- Customers are likely to go through five stages in their journey with your business from discovering you, to becoming interested, to evaluating your offer against alternatives, to purchase and ultimately to review and, hopefully, recommendation
- It's important to identify which are the critical points in the journey that will be your 'moments of truth'

To get you thinking...

- What are the critical factors in your customer's journey, your moments of truth?
- Where are there opportunities to differentiate your business from your competitors?

Action points...

- Use the workbook to map your customer's journey through your business
- Identify the moments of truth in your customer's journey and work out how to ensure you get these right every time
- Think how you will gather feedback and testimonials from customers

Part **3**

Getting started

Chapter **11**

Promoting your business

'The best marketing doesn't feel like marketing.'
—Tom Fishburne

Your ideal client is not going to beat a path to your door just because you opened it! You are going to have to work at getting your message in front of them in a way that will appeal and move them through your sales funnel. Your sales funnel is the marketing process that will progress your ideal client from stranger to fan; it is very closely tied with the customer journey we looked at in the last chapter.

The Sales Funnel

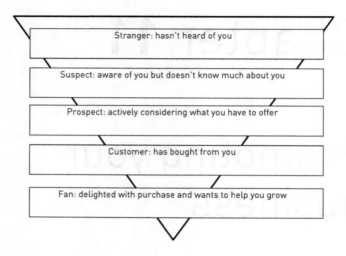

Your first challenge is to make your ideal customer aware that you exist; you then have to get their interest, after which you want them to understand how you can help them and to encourage them to try you out. Once they've tried you out you want them to purchase and then, if you've really got it right they'll become a fan and start telling others about you. So your marketing activities and your message need to be appropriate to the point your target is at. We started to examine the tactics you might use in the last chapter; in this one we're going to look at how to use each of the tactics effectively.

Understanding your prospect

By now you should have quite a good understanding about your ideal customer, the pain that you will solve for them and the triggers that will encourage them to buy. However, before you craft your marketing messages there are a few more things you need to consider.

Your prospect is better informed than he has ever been. He has access to advice 24/7 and may well be suffering from information overload. He may have lost sight of what is really important. He may be fed up with hype and false promises. On the other hand, he has probably identified his alternatives, may feel he understands their features and benefits and may have a view on relative prices and value. Your challenge is to help him to a reach a decision and of course the decision you want is for him to choose you.

You also need to think who is going to influence that decision. In some instances the customer – the person who buys – is not the same as the consumer – the person who uses. Remember buying clothes for your child, you thought they were the bee's knees but your child refused to wear them because they just weren't cool? You need to make sure that you understand how your prospect will arrive at a buying decision and who will influence it and make sure that your marketing addresses the right people with the right information. That can mean that it has to address two or more audiences.

If you are selling your services to another business you will need to identify that business' decision-making process. It is all too easy to waste hours wooing a person who has no power to buy. It's therefore important that one of the first questions you ask is what the company's buying procedure is and who you need to influence.

Crafting your message

Getting your marketing message right is tricky, getting it wrong is really easy and many people do! These are some common mistakes you should try to avoid:

- Promotional material just lists features without explaining the benefits to the target audience
- The target audience is unclear so the message doesn't get attention
- The message is too 'we we'; in other words it's blatant self-promotion that doesn't engage with the prospect
- There is no call to action so the prospect doesn't know what to do next
- Vital information is missing, things like phone number, address or opening hours

- There's too much emphasis on the business name rather than a headline that will engage the prospect

How you craft your message will depend upon the message itself, the medium and the audience but there are some basic principles to follow. Marketers have long used the mnemonic AIDA as a planning and copywriting tool, it's a great way to check that you haven't made any of the mistakes above. So what does it stand for?

- **A**ttention
- **I**nterest
- **D**esire
- **A**ction

A more recent addition has been C for **C**onviction given the more informed audience we are now addressing.

Let's consider this principle in a bit more detail.

Gaining attention

If your message doesn't attract the attention of your target audience you are wasting your time and money. Given how much information we are constantly bombarded with you have a few seconds at most to gain attention. Think about the fliers that pop through the letter box, yours has to gain your target's attention in the distance it takes from the letter box to the recycling bin. The email's subject line has to persuade you to open it before you click the delete key.

An eye-catching image can help but your headline or subject line is vital. You want something that stops your target in his tracks and makes him read on. Ideally your headline will pinpoint the problem you are trying to solve and if you can raise his curiosity better still. That's why a question often works. Our natural response to a question is to answer it so if your question can get your target to recognise that your message is addressed to him you have a good chance that he will read on. Here are some ideas that you could adapt (change the words in italics to suit you):

- What's the solution to *your never-ending 'to do' list*?
- How can you *lose weight without being hungry*?
- Is it possible to *get your new baby to sleep all night*?
- Where can you find *a steady stream of customers ready to do business with you*?
- What would you do if *your main fuse blew at 7.30p.m.*?

Your headline wants to 'speak' to your target so using words like 'you' or 'your' personalises it and can help gain attention. Numbers, especially odd ones, also attract attention. For example:

- 5 ways to save money on your gas bill
- 3 tips to cut your to-do list in half
- Cut your costs by up to 37%

Professional copywriters will typically spend somewhere between 50% and 70% of the project time crafting the headline. They may brainstorm 50 or more alternatives before whittling them down to a handful that could work. If it takes a professional so much effort it's unlikely that you will get to a great headline in 10 minutes so give yourself time to develop your thoughts. Most professionals keep a swipe file of ideas that have caught their attention. This can be really helpful. You don't want to copy someone else's work but you can be inspired by it so why not start a swipe file of your own? As you look through the contents you will probably find a number of formulae that appear again and again, there's a reason... they work. Don't feel that you have to reinvent the wheel all the time.

Generating interest

Once you've got your target's attention then your aim should be to get their interest. Your headline may have identified their pain so now you have to make them really feel the agony. It's time to rub a bit of salt into the wound!

Go back to your list of all the pain points you identified in thinking about your target market. Describe them in a way that your ideal client will feel them and then offer a solution. Let's think about our stressed out 40-year-old mum, remember her?

167

She's juggling a family, career, home and social life. She's reached breaking point, she can't sleep, she's got a constant headache, she's snapping at everyone, she's either not eating or overeating and she may be drinking too much. Our marketing message has to make her feel all of these things to the point where she *really* wants to find a solution.

So your headline might be:

- When did you last get a good night's sleep?

Or

- Do you feel like you could snap at any minute?

You could follow this up with something like:

Are you worn out juggling work, family, home and a million and one other things, so you just don't have enough hours in the day? You're pushing yourself, constantly working all hours, sleep is a luxury you don't have time for so you've got a constant niggling headache and a feeling of overwhelm. How would you feel if you could just get a great night's sleep and lose that headache?

Now you have some interest it's time to make her want your solution.

Creating desire

Now is the time to explain your solution by describing what it is and how it helps your target. This means talking about features... what it is... and benefits... what's this means to your prospect.

Let's look at some examples:

- Food delivered to your door (feature) so you don't have to waste time on a supermarket trip (benefit)
- The zip-off clutch bag (feature) means that you'll only ever need to take one bag on a business trip (benefit)
- 100% money back guarantee backed by *** (feature) so you can be totally confident that your purchase is risk free (benefit)

The trick is to match the features and benefits to the particular target you have in your sights and to make sure that they help that person to take the next step.

So a stranger needs to understand why they should click on your website or call into your shop whereas a prospect should be given reasons for buying.

Going back to our 40 year old wanting to get a good night's sleep, the massage therapist might say:

- Our deep tissue massage will release tension in your muscles leaving you feeling relaxed and at peace with the world. Many clients report that they sleep so much better after a treatment.

In this example we've got the feature... deep tissue massage, the benefit... feeling relaxed and at peace, and a little bit of conviction... other clients report... A testimonial from a client like our 40 year old would reinforce the conviction.

Take a look at some of the marketing material that has converted you, what was it that persuaded you to take action? Look particularly at those things that you bought which you probably didn't need but bought because you wanted them. Something such as my 'fabulous new work bag', for instance. Did I need a new work bag? No. Was I looking for a new work bag? No. So why did I buy it? I bought it because the marketing hit all my buttons; it allowed me to persuade myself that I had the problems the bag was designed to solve. I recognised myself as the businesswoman struggling with briefcase and handbag. I craved the organisation it offered where there was a slot for everything that usually lurks at the bottom of my bag. I loved that my computer would fit in its own spot and that there was a bag for my charging leads. I've found myself having to buy a plastic carrier in the convenience store when I popped in on the way home from work so the built-in shopping bag really appealed. I was sold when I could have it in teal, my favourite colour and my brand identity. It allows me to portray the image of the success I wish to be.

The more you understand about your ideal client and the things that matter to them the better your marketing materials will become as you engage with her self-talk. When you know what matters to her you will speak to her in a way that really engages and has her keen to do business with you.

Reassuring your prospect (Conviction)

Your loyal customers already know, like and trust you so they don't really need any reassurance however a new customer is taking a risk and they want to know it is a calculated one. Testimonials can help, especially if the person giving the testimonial resembles your target; this is why video testimonials can be so powerful. Your prospect wants to know that the testimonial is genuine and not just more marketing hype.

Guarantees, especially those backed by a third party, make it easier for new customers to take the risk. Another option is a try before you buy offer.

How you incorporate this element into your marketing will depend on the medium and the point in the funnel that your prospect is at, the closer to purchase that they are the more it becomes relevant.

Your call to action

It's vital that your message tells your interested prospect what you want them to do next. Make it as easy as possible and use an action verb. Here are some ideas:

- Call
- Visit
- Book
- Email
- Ring
- Click
- Download
- Try
- Test
- Order
- Buy now

Choose the call to action that is most relevant to the stage of the customer journey that your prospect is at. Don't confuse them by giving them options. For example, if you invite them to call or email this will cause them to have to make a decision and might delay, or even prevent, them from taking action. This does not mean that you don't share more than one means of contacting you. So include your phone, email and website address for example in case your website crashes with the volume of hits your marketing generates or there is a problem with your phone or emails. You don't want to lose a prospect who is keen to take action because they can't find another means of contacting you. However, one call to action allows you to prepare for handling the response, for example by setting up automatic responses to emails or bringing in extra help to staff the phones.

Choosing your voice

In chapter 8 we talked about your brand's tone of voice and this is never more relevant than in your marketing material. This is the place where you can control your tone so take care that your messages are consistent and on brand.

Many businesses fall into the trap I called too much 'we we', where they talk about 'we do this', 'we do that', 'our this' and 'our that'. Your prospect isn't interested in you and what matters to you, their interests are much more self-centred! Try to find a way to talk from your prospect's point of view and use you and your rather than we and our. A good rule of thumb is 70% you and 30% we. If you have to use we make sure that you make it relevant to your prospect, for example, we're open from 7.00a.m. to 9.00p.m. so that you can shop on your way to or from work.

One trick that works for many copywriters is to design an avatar of the target reader. So describe your ideal client and give her a name and then write to her and just her. This will make your marketing material much more human and engaging. So your avatar might look like this:

Susan is a 50-year-old mother of two. She had a successful corporate career in management before having her first child

18 years ago. Since then she has been a stay at home mum. She's a school governor and an active volunteer in her own community. Now that her children are nearing adulthood she wants to start her own business based from home. She's got a business idea but doesn't know how to bring it to fruition. She's risk averse so wants to learn as much as she can before starting. Her three biggest concerns are: making a profit, winning customers and managing her time.

Or

Bob is approaching retirement from the police. Although he'll leave with a pension he worries that it will not be enough to support his teenage children who will be going to university soon. He also worries that he'll be bored and that his life will lack meaning without the structure and status his work gives him.

When you have more than one target market you will need more than one avatar and, generally, separate marketing messages for each. The avatar will enable you to pitch your marketing at the right level and to use the right triggers to get your target to take the action you want.

If you are going to outsource your marketing your copywriter will find the avatar really helpful but will also want to understand your brand and know about the features and benefits of your products and services.

Testing

It's a good idea to run some controlled tests with your marketing materials. Measure the responses you get, how many people take the action you invited? How many move to the next stage of your sales funnel? How many people buy? Then tweak one thing and measure again. Maybe try a different headline or change your call to action or try different benefits to see which get the best results. But only change one thing at a time otherwise you won't know what worked better or less well.

Keep copies of your marketing material with the statistics so that you have all the information you need when you are comparing performance.

Choosing your tactics

So far in this chapter we've considered some general principles, now we're going to look at some of the marketing activities that you might use in your business. You will not be able to do everything so you will need to identify those that will be most likely to reach your ideal client. For example, it's no good spending all your time on LinkedIn if your target is only on Facebook. It's no good sponsoring a local event if it is of no interest to your prospect or their connections. The key is to choose a limited number of activities and do them regularly and consistently, and then you can experiment with other options when you have time and money.

People rarely buy on the first contact so you will need to think how you can get your message to your ideal client in multiple ways without being annoying. It is often said that your message needs to be seen six to eight times before someone will take action; it can be more. This is something you should measure in your own business. People will buy when they are ready to buy so you need to stay in touch for when that day comes. One of my best clients had known me for nearly 20 years before she decided that she needed my services!

Online

It is my belief that every business needs an online presence, even if the business is a hyper-local bricks and mortar establishment. What do you do when you are looking for a new product or service? I'll bet that in nine out of ten cases you start with Google or Facebook, on the tenth occasion you might ask a friend. Your prospects do the same. If they can't find you on Google they'll probably go to your competitor who does have a presence. Perhaps a friend or someone in a Facebook group will recommend you and give your email or phone number. However, the chances are the prospect would like to check you out before they contact you and if they can't do that online they may take another recommendation that did have a web presence.

So what are your options?

- *Website*: this doesn't have to be hugely expensive. These days there are a wide variety of flexible, templated, build your own options that don't require a vast amount of technical expertise. If you don't want to go the DIY route then it doesn't need to cost a fortune to get a web developer to build the site for you. Websites get expensive when they are bespoke and complex so if you keep it simple you can keep down the costs. A one-page site may be all you need to enable your prospect to find you online.

The beauty of a website is that you have control. You choose the look, the content and how people interact with it. Your website may even offer you a supplementary route to market allowing customers to order or book online.

- *Social media:* some successful businesses have been built entirely on the strength of social media. For example, many skilled craftspeople use their Facebook page as their primary promotional tool. They have built a large following often by sharing each other's pages. They keep that audience engaged by posting regularly, showing new work and promoting their attendance at markets and fairs. Many use competitions to build their following and keep their followers engaged.

The downside of social media is that you are subject to the whims and business decisions of the channel owners. If Facebook decided that you had broken their rules you may lose access to all your followers. When they decide that they want you to pay for advertising they can change their algorithms so that less people see your free posts.

Your use of social media should depend upon your target market and their use of it. You need to be where they hang out. This is something you need to keep under constant review as new channels emerge and people change their behaviour. In the early days mainly younger people used Facebook but now it is used more by women in their 40s and 50s, and young people have moved on. LinkedIn is seen as the professional, more corporate platform. Instagram, Pinterest and Snapchat tend to be more visual image sharing sites. Video is becoming more and more important so social media platforms are introducing live streaming and recorded videos allowing you to engage with your audience directly.

A big advantage of social media is the ability to target your message to your ideal customer. For a relatively low fee you can choose precisely who sees your advertising message, which is great when you are targeting a clearly defined local market.

If all this makes you throw up your hands in horror, social media doesn't have to be scary or take over your life. There are numerous social media experts who will train you how best to use it or will even do it for you. If you are new to social media don't try to be everywhere at once. Hopefully your research will have told you which social media channels your ideal customer uses most frequently so concentrate on understanding that one. Set yourself up with an account (get help if you need it) and follow a few people in your network. Look out for free or low-cost training on your chosen platform. Learn by observation and by engaging with the people you know until you are confident to promote yourself and your business.

- *Blogging:* if you want to demonstrate your knowledge or skill then blogging can be a great way to do it. If blogging is a mystery to you then a blog is an online diary or collection of conversational style articles. You can add a blog section to your website or have a standalone site. By posting regularly you can show the breadth of your expertise and talents. You can choose to post articles, pictures or video and build a following of people interested in what you do. This can be particularly effective for service-based businesses where skill and expertise are what you are selling. Include a call to action to make the most of your blog.

If you are on a really tight budget you can even blog for free, if you are willing to include the blog host's name in your domain, or a small fee will allow you a domain without it. For years I blogged at www.thetrainingpack.wordpress.com without it costing me a penny. My blog has been really useful in helping to convert prospects into customers.

- *Video:* there are many who say video is the future, it already accounts for about one third of time spent online and the statistics for the contribution video makes to conversion are impressive. The beauty of video is that it enables people who don't know you to see what you're like and also enables you to showcase your skill and expertise.

Whether you have your own YouTube channel, use live streaming such as Facebook Live or Periscope or simply use video on your website it is something you should consider.

- *Webinars:* are another great tool for showcasing your expertise (if you are unfamiliar with the term, a webinar is, in effect, an online class or seminar). Webinars are very much a tool of choice for many online businesses in the knowledge field but they work well for locally based businesses too. The idea is that you deliver content that is of value to your target audience to act as a taster for a more in-depth sold programme. This could be a workshop or training course or one to one coaching for example.

- *Directories:* would your ideal client look for your service in an online directory? Perhaps your professional body has a searchable list of accredited consultants or maybe there is a list for your industry.

Online works for a local business...

*A personal training studio may be the epitome of a local business but **Roy Summers** has found that his most effective marketing tool is the Bodyline Fitness website. He works hard to keep the website up to date and close to the top of Google page one for the search terms his clients are likely to use.*

Roy regularly posts new content, especially blogs, but also new features and newsletters. This all helps maintain his Google ranking.

Directories bring in new business...

***Alastair Lyon** of IFA Direct lists his services and contact details in a couple of online directories specific to his industry. The directories contribute a steady flow of enquiries, which supplement the leads that Alastair generates through his networking and other marketing activities.*

Marketing materials

You will need to think about what kind of marketing materials you need. Look at the customer journey that you mapped out in the last chapter, what are the touch points where materials will help? For instance, if you plan to network, you will certainly need a business card and maybe a flier or pop-up banner.

- *Business card:* don't overlook the marketing potential of your business card. It can be one of the most cost effective tools you use. It's a good idea to include your website and key social media details as well as your name and contact information but also think how you can include a marketing message. You may find that a folded card would give you more space. There are those who believe that a photo is a good idea, as it will help people to remember you. It may also be helpful to leave a small amount of white space for your new contact to make a note to remind them how they met you or what you agreed. In some enterprises the business card can double as an appointment card.

- *Fliers and leaflets:* for many locally based businesses leaflet drops can be an effective way to raise awareness. A 2–3% response rate is a reasonable expectation but if you are able to be really targeted and have a great offer you may get this up to 5%. Fliers can also be useful for people to pick up at events you attend, especially if you have the sort of business that is not a routine spend.

Read the information on crafting your message to ensure that you don't make the mistakes so many make with their materials. Remember fliers are like toast, if you only print on one side then it will land butter side down and your prospect may not even see your message before it hits the recycling bin. I have found that an A6 postcard with an attention grabbing picture and headline on one side, and a benefits-laden message on the other has worked well for my clients. Don't forget your call to action. The beauty of an attractive postcard is that your target is more likely to retain it, perhaps pinned on the fridge, so your message has more chance to hit the spot.

- *Brochures:* if your offer is complex or you have a range of products to sell then a brochure can be quite useful. However, these can be quite costly so take care how many you print if the products or prices are likely to change frequently. You may do better with a flier that invites people to check out your website.

Targeted marketing

The more directly you can target your marketing the more likely it is to be successful. These days *email marketing* and *newsletters* are amongst the most popular methods of reaching, and staying in touch with, your market. However, there is a danger that your target's inbox will be overloaded so you will need to have a really good subject line and a message that not only fits with the subject line but also appeals to the recipient. Emails that offer your target something they will value will be more likely to be opened and read. Do remember that you need to have permission to send marketing emails and will also need to make it clear how people can unsubscribe from your mailing list.

Direct mail used to be much more popular than it is now but it can still be very effective. Direct mail usually consists of a letter to a named individual whereas a *mailshot* is a less personalised attempt at reaching a wider audience. One way to get attention for your mailing is to include a sample or free gift. I've been sent a tea bag and invited to make myself a cup whilst I peruse the letter, pens that enable me to sample the product and cup mats that keep the business' details in front of me for as long as I use it. Obviously there is a cost involved with this, not to mention the postage, but as part of an integrated marketing campaign they can be very effective. The trick is to make the letter as personalised as possible using the AIDCA principle described earlier.

Many of us hate marketing on the *telephone* but done well it can be very effective because it allows you to engage your target in conversation and to get up close and personal with your offer. If you integrate the phone call with your direct mail campaign you increase the chances of success. You could write in the first instance and in the letter say you will call in the next few days. When you ring you ask if the person has received your letter and if they have any queries.

Alternatively, you can call first to explore whether your target has any interest in your service and to gain a good understanding of the issues they have. You can then follow up with a really personalised offer contained in a letter.

A word of warning! You must stay on the right side of the law when marketing directly to people. Recipients of your marketing emails should have opted into receiving them from you unless they have bought a similar product from you recently; even then it's a good idea to check they are happy to receive your newsletter. You can invite people to join your mailing list via your website, often with an inducement of a useful download such as a checklist or ask them to tick that they give permission on a pro forma or contact details card. You should always make it easy for people to unsubscribe from your list. Don't take it personally, your target may prefer to connect with you on social media in order to maintain control of their inbox and it's much better to have a smaller list of willing recipients than a big list of people who rarely open your emails. Don't be tempted to sell or share your list with anyone else unless you made it clear that you would do so when you were seeking permission from the individuals on the list.

You should always check whether the person you are calling is registered with the Telephone Preference Service (http://www.tpsonline.org.uk/) and if they are don't call unless you have their specific permission to do so. For direct mail you should check out the Mailing Preference Service (www.mpsonline.org.uk), this will help you to avoid mailing someone who has opted out of marketing emails but it can be particularly helpful in stopping you writing to someone who is recently deceased.

Most small businesses will build their own marketing lists from people they have met or who have made an enquiry but you might decide to buy a mailing list from a database holder. Do check that the list has been obtained via legal methods. If you do buy a list make sure that you use it within the terms of the agreement, if you buy a single-use list (not a good idea) then the only people you can send a second communication to are those who responded to your first message. The list owner will have a means of checking that you are using the list as agreed. If you are going to buy a list buy it for multiple use so that you can communicate often enough to move a proportion of the recipients through your marketing funnel.

Sponsorship

If you want to build a name and reputation locally sponsorship can be one way to do it. You could support a school fete, sponsor a local sports team or back a local event. Before you agree to part with any money think how the deal fits with your marketing strategy. Who will benefit from your support? Will your target audience hear about your commitment? Is the opportunity in line with your brand values?

For sponsorship to work it needs to raise your profile so you need to be able to put your business name, logo and marketing message in front of your target audience. If you can't do that you are making a donation rather than sponsoring.

Be very clear what you want to get out of the sponsorship deal and make that a part of your negotiations. Don't forget to make the most of PR by targeting local media for coverage.

Exhibiting

Exhibitions can be fun and a great way to get in front of many of your target audience at one event but they can also be an expensive waste of time. Before you book, check what kind of exhibition it's going to be. Who is the target audience and is it right for you? How will the organisers attract and keep visitors at the expo? Who else will be exhibiting and will there be too many direct competitors? Will you have access to visitor contact details so that you can follow up even with those you didn't have chance to speak to?

Work out all the costs of exhibiting... expo fee, your stand, your marketing material and any giveaways, your time and any help you might need to pay for, transport and parking. How many customers will you need to win to make it worth the investment? How many leads will you need to get to that many customers and are you likely to be able to speak to so many people?

If you do decide to exhibit make sure that you allow sufficient time for preparation and even more for follow-up. It's the follow-up that is the most vital element.

Advertising

Many small business owners waste hundreds, if not thousands, of pounds on advertising. If you are going to consider advertising there are lots of things you need to think about before booking your space:

- Will the advert reach enough of your target market to make it worth the investment?

- Research suggests that your target needs to see the ad between six and eight times before it even registers; will that happen in your chosen medium? If you advertise on the back of a bus on a busy local route then if your target market is a local driver there is a good chance that, at some point, they will take notice of your advertisement as they sit behind the bus in a traffic queue. However, as they will be driving you need to make sure that the call to action is very easy to remember. An easy website will probably be more effective than a phone number unless you are lucky enough to be able to get a number that is an easily retained pattern. Advertising in a newspaper or magazine that is read once and then binned is unlikely to work unless you book a series of ads running over several issues or running on multiple pages. The exception is an advert for a service that someone looks for in the local paper, so something like a man with a van or car servicing.
- Ask for a media pack to see the reach of the publication and its target market. Check how easy it will be to target your advert to the right people. If you are advertising a premium service you probably don't want to pay to cover the whole of town but want to reach those in the higher value homes.
- Don't pay the rate on the card without negotiating. In most cases the rate is a starting point and you will often be able to get a much better deal especially if you book multiple adverts or if you wait until the publishing deadline is imminent. The exception can be the hyper-local publications which are published on a shoestring and where rates are often very low, even then you may be able to get a deal on multiple bookings
- A flier inserted into a newspaper or magazine is often more effective than on-page advertising as people will see it when it falls out but may skip past adverts in the body of the publication. It's also easier to target loose inserts than on-page advertising, as the distributor will include it for the postcodes you select.
- Creating an effective advert is a skill given the very limited space you have available. You'll need to apply the AIDCA

principles but think how they will work in the medium you are working with. For example, if you are advertising in a newspaper the reproduction quality on a photo may not give you the impact you need. White space tends to be more important in a newspaper ad.

Public Relations

According to the Chartered Institute of Public Relations 'Public Relations is about reputation – the result of what you do, what you say and what others say about you.' You may think of it in terms of managing your brand and especially those harder to control elements below the waterline.

For a small, locally based business, managing your public relations probably means building relationships with local journalists and other local influencers. If you can make a journalist's life easier by supplying them with a good local story of interest to their target reader then you may well find yourself in the local paper or on local TV. The essential ingredient is a good story not a sales pitch. A new product launch is unlikely to capture the journalist's attention unless you do something exciting to launch it. You could take some lessons from Richard Branson who has been known to abseil down a building to launch a new flight route.

You may be able to generate interest in your business launch from your backstory. For example, it took a cardiac arrest for Jane Hardy, MD of Fabulous Women and Marvellous Men, to give up the corporate life in favour of running her own business. That's a pretty dramatic story that might capture a journalist's attention.

An event or sponsorship deal is also a good PR opportunity so we'll consider that when we talk about how to launch your business in chapter 14.

Point of sale

The material you display at the point of sale can have significant influence on your customer's buying behaviour. If you are selling products then a display, or sales promotional material, which shows how one product can be combined with others can result in an upsell. Take a lesson from the major retailers and think about multiple purchase offers such as buy a shirt and get the tie for half price, buy a cleanser and get 20% off the eye make-up remover. How could you adapt the McDonald's, 'Would you like fries with that?' message?

Point of sale doesn't just apply to retail businesses. Does the client who has booked a facial with you know that you also do pedicures? Would a course attendee welcome a follow-up one to one or be ready for a more advanced course in a few weeks' time? Would your customer welcome a valet clean with their car service?

Your customer is often most receptive to spending money when they've already decided to buy. So think carefully about how you can encourage them to spend more at this point without making them feel uncomfortable or bullied into spending more than they wanted to. Your aim is to have the customer feeling delighted that you have supplied them with exactly what they wanted.

Networking

You will probably come across business owners who say that networking doesn't work. I couldn't disagree more! When it doesn't work it's usually because the person expected instant results. Networking is a long game but for many locally based small businesses it can be *the* most effective marketing channel. It works primarily in two ways. Firstly, the people you meet whilst networking may become your customers. Secondly, when you have established a strong relationship with the people in your network they can become your sales team.

There are numerous networking organisations to choose from, from business breakfasts, mid-morning groups to lunch, early evening and dinner clubs. Some offer structured networking with opportunities to present your business to the whole room whilst others are more informal with the opportunity to work the room chatting to individuals. Then there are those that combine networking with another activity such as walking or golf. You will need to choose what works for you. Some groups are open to all, some restrict the number of people from a profession and some are by invitation only.

I suggest visiting groups you might be interested in joining, most groups will be pleased to invite you either to a visitors' day or a regular meeting. See what kind of people are there and how the meeting works. Remember that your target client may not be in the room but may be very well connected with the people who are. That's why it's really important to help people to understand what you do, who you do it for and what would help you. That's when your marketing materials can be really helpful.

The chances are that the connections you make at regular meetings will be relatively superficial so make some time for one to one meetings so you can get to know each other better and explore ways that you can help each other. Follow up with the new people that you meet but don't add them to your mailing list without their express permission.

You will get the most from networking when you commit to it in the long term and when you take a structured approach to it. Many regular networkers say that networking has really helped them to clarify what their business is all about. When you have to do a one-minute pitch to the same audience every week or month it really makes you think about your message. The questions that people ask you at the one to ones can help you to refine that message.

When you choose the right networking organisation the benefits can be much greater than just new business. You make friends in business, which is really helpful when you are a solopreneur. The opportunity to bounce ideas around, to share challenges and successes is invaluable. Choose your organisations carefully and be sure to choose one that will be right for you. Some organisations are strict about not admitting competing businesses but others support collaboration so what will help you to grow your business?

An integrated marketing plan...

As was demonstrated in the customer journey in the last chapter Fabulous Women and Marvellous Men has an integrated marketing plan. This consists of online through the website, directory listings and social media activity supplemented by

> *posters, marketing material and exhibitions to reach local business owners in a targeted area. The organisation will also use press releases when appropriate and the most successful Group Leaders regularly network with other organisations in their area.*

Marketing regularly

Whatever marketing activities you choose you will need to do them consistently and regularly. You can't just turn on the tap and expect new customers to gush out. It takes time to build relationships that lead to sales. Remember that people will typically need to hear from you six to eight times to take notice. If you only turn on the marketing taps when you are short of customers your business will be full of peaks and troughs. If you can't spare the time to do regular marketing yourself outsource it or automate it.

You want a marketing plan that is integrated and leads your prospect through your marketing funnel seamlessly. That might mean networking to raise awareness, one to ones to generate interest and trial sessions to aid decision making. When you've delivered the service you should ask for feedback and, if all is well, ask for a referral, which will move perhaps to a direct mail letter to raise awareness and to an email newsletter to stay in touch with your happy customer.

Alternatively, you might generate awareness through your website or social media presence, invite your prospect to download a checklist or informative guide and then follow up with an invitation to an event.

As you have seen there is a vast range of tools to choose from. Don't be tempted to try to use them all. Effectiveness comes from consistency so it is better to restrict yourself to a handful of tools that you use regularly and well rather than using a scattergun that never hits your target. It's important to measure your results and amend your plan accordingly; we discuss this in chapter 13.

There's an exercise in your workbook to help you to plan your marketing activities alongside your customer's journey and your marketing funnel.

In summary...

- Your marketing activity should be based on a thorough understanding of your target customer and their reasons for buying your product or service
- Your marketing messages need to be crafted to attract attention and move your prospect towards buying and they should include a clear call to action
- There are multiple online and offline marketing tools at your disposal. Your challenge is to select a number of tools that you can manage and that will win you business

To get you thinking...

- When have you taken action as a direct result of marketing? What was it that made you take that action and could you use that in your business?
- How many marketing activities can you maintain effectively?

Action points...

- Complete the AIDCA planning document in the workbook

- Visit a number of local networking groups to assess their potential to work for you and your business
- Revisit the results of your market research to identify how your ideal clients choose a new supplier. Use the results to identify three to five marketing activities that you will do regularly.

Chapter **12**

Getting Help

'Be strong enough to stand alone, smart enough to know when you need help, and brave enough to ask for it.'
—Mark Amend

As we discussed in chapter 4 it can be tempting, when starting out, to try to do everything ourselves but this can be a false economy. Remember that you may be losing money for every hour that you spend on a task that someone else could do for less money than you would charge a client for that hour. What's more, an expert may get a task done in an hour that would take you most of the day. It's also worth remembering that once we are past 40 we may not have quite as much energy or stamina as we did at 21 and getting help can leave us able to give quality time to the tasks that only we can do.

What kind of help could be useful?

 Make a list of all the different activities that will need to happen if your business is to succeed. Here are some ideas to get you started:

- Marketing including website maintenance, newsletters, promotional materials, social media etc.
- Networking
- Selling
- Customer service
- Complaints management
- Proposal documents
- Presentations
- Events management
- Contracts and agreements
- Production
- Delivery of services
- Invoicing
- Bookkeeping
- Tax returns
- Diary management
- Travel arrangements
- Vehicle and equipment maintenance
- Purchasing and supplier relationships
- Quality control
- Research and development
- Business planning
- Recruitment
- Training and personal development
- Payroll
- Personnel management

Some of these tasks take a lot of time and need to be done regularly so are you the best person to do them?

Outsourcing tasks

One of the most flexible ways to get jobs done is to outsource them, for example to a virtual assistant (VA) or a bookkeeper. But it's important to choose the right person for the job and be really clear about your expectations and agreements.

The services offered by one virtual assistant might be very different from those offered by another. Some offer traditional personal assistant services such as diary management, typing and travel bookings whereas others may be more of a marketing assistant and offer copywriting, newsletter production, social media and website maintenance. What do you need a VA to do? Do you need regular support or a one-off project? Can you cope with remote help or do you need face to face contact or physical help?

Once you know what sort of help you are looking for ask your network for recommendations, check out a few websites or post your task on one of the outsourcing websites, see www.foundedafter40.co.uk for suggestions. Whichever way you find the assistance do your homework to make sure that candidates have the ability to deliver the results you need.

Check out the quality of the work your potential assistant produces. Can they spell and write grammatically? Do they deliver to deadlines? Do they have the expertise to deliver right first time without too much management from you? Will they create the right impression with your clients and prospects?

Once you have chosen the right person, negotiate an agreement that works for both of you. Many virtual assistants have standard terms of business, do these work for you or do you need to adapt them? The agreement may relate to standard packages so make sure you put the work you need doing and any essential milestones and deadlines in writing – an email is fine. Remember that people's perception of your brand will be affected just as much by the work other people do in your name as the work you do yourself. Set your expectations at the outset and make sure your agreement covers amendments, revisions or what happens if the standard of work produced is not acceptable.

Manage the project. Be available to deal with queries. Sample the work in progress before too much time is used producing work that isn't quite what you were hoping for. Make sure that the milestones are being met. Invest time in developing the relationship, especially if you expect it to be ongoing.

Building a team...

Roy Summers has grown his Bodyline Fitness business by building a team. Specific tasks such as accounting and design are outsourced to suitably qualified professionals with whom Roy has developed an ongoing and constructive relationship. By recruiting a team of self-employed trainers who pay to use the studio Roy has also created an income that does not rely exclusively on him selling time for money. This means that Roy is able to take time away from the business on a regular basis to work on marketing and business development. Roy has also sold a small share of the business to one of his trusted trainers so now has a sounding board for ideas and also someone to share the decision making and responsibilities with.

Jane Hardy of Fabulous Women and Marvellous Men has ready access to help and support from within her network. She outsources financial management, administration and marketing on a routine basis but is also able to access coaching, design and other skills as and when needed. This gives Jane access to a wide range of skills and experience from people who care about her and her business. She has a ready sounding board for ideas from people she trusts to challenge her as well as support her.

Are you the right person for the job?

Sometimes we outsource because we're overloaded and sometimes because someone else can do a better job than we can. Should you be outsourcing the tasks you don't enjoy or are not good at? Could you use other people's skills and contacts to meet your needs? For instance, you may find a sales representative or agent who would achieve a much greater level of sales than you can. Think about it: most actors don't go touting themselves to producers or directors; they use an agent. That agent represents a number of artists and therefore has established relationships with the producers and directors who will contact the agent when they are looking to fill a particular role.

If you are a greetings card designer then you should be able to find a sales representative who would like to add your designs to his portfolio. He'll have relationships with a range of card shops, often independents, and will be able to match your designs to the shops where they will sell best. The retailer will like the arrangement because they get a wider choice of designs without having to make time to see every individual designer, the agent likes it because he gets a percentage from each of his designers whilst also keeping the retailers happy and you like it because you can concentrate on designing.

If you are looking for this kind of help in your industry it can be worth starting with your industry body which should be able to put you in touch with a range of people who meet your brief. If your own trade association can't help look for organisations that the person you are looking for might belong to. For example, if you want a lawyer then the Law Society may be able to help. Alternatively, you can try an internet search but take care to do your due diligence to ensure that the person you have found is suitable and has appropriate qualifications.

Employing staff

Taking on your first employee is a big commitment but may be essential if you have a business that needs someone available for long hours. For instance, if you have a bricks and mortar business that is open six or seven days a week you will almost certainly need at least one part-time employee. Don't be tempted to rely on volunteer help from friends and family, it rarely works in the long term. Whilst your friends and family will probably be happy to help you on occasion they do have lives and commitments of their own and when you are not paying them these are bound to take priority from time to time.

Recruiting the right team can be challenging...

*When **Buki Obakin** opened her childrenswear boutique, Finoora, recruiting and retaining staff with the skills needed to work with minimum supervision was one of her greatest challenges. With a shop open six days a week and a retail website to manage Buki needed reliable staff with good customer service, IT and stock management skills. This proved challenging and Buki found herself having to work more hours in the shop than she really wanted to.*

 Getting the right people for the right job at the right time is essential so it is worth taking time to think carefully about what you need. If you don't have any experience in human resource management or recruitment it might be worth paying for professional help. At the very least you should take a professional approach to recruitment because mistakes can be time consuming and costly.

Job descriptions

Exactly what do you want your employee to do? What's the job's purpose? What are the key duties and responsibilities? Check that the duties and responsibilities are consistent. For example, if you say the job's purpose is to deputise for the owner and then list only routine tasks with no management responsibility you are unlikely to attract the right candidate. Of course in a small start-up you probably want someone who will turn their hand to anything, just as you will do, but if you want a deputy you need someone who will be capable of taking decisions and working on their own initiative. When you know what is involved then you can give the job a title but again take care not to overhype or you will not attract the ideal candidate. Try to keep your job description relatively broad to retain flexibility and avoid challenges when you ask your new employee to undertake a task not explicitly mentioned. It's usual to include a reporting structure in a job description to make it absolutely clear what the decision-making channels are. This can be particularly helpful if you are a partnership or have more than one employee.

There is a job description template in your workbook.

Person specifications

What skills, qualities and experience will be required to do this job successfully? Typically these are grouped into essential and desirable headings. Take care that your choice of wording does not make your specification discriminatory. This can happen quite inadvertently for example when specifying qualifications when it might be better to say, 'GCSE English or equivalent' so that you don't discriminate against people who were not educated in the UK system. Does the wording imply that you are seeking someone of a particular age or gender for example? Can you justify your reasons for stipulating certain experience or could it be interpreted as discriminatory on age?

How will you select the right candidate?

Selecting the right candidate is no easy task. You've probably encountered the brilliant interviewee who turns out to be all talk and no action or maybe you've taken a punt on a gibbering wreck to find they become a brilliant employee. Is an interview the best way to choose the right person for the job? In my extensive recruitment experience I would suggest that an interview on its own is not. So try to design your recruitment process to test as many of the essential qualities as you can.

For example, if you need someone to take phone calls make the first part of the selection process a telephone interview. How good is the applicant at introducing themselves? What impression do they convey on the phone? Do they speak clearly and professionally? If you want someone to support you with administration set them an admin task, perhaps an in-tray exercise (a list of activities that they have to prioritise). If you want someone to write letters get them to write a letter of application but don't assume that the letter of application was written in a timely manner without help. Set them a letter-writing task as part of the selection process. If you want someone who can sell ask them to sell something to you and don't be afraid to be a rather awkward customer.

When you have your job description, person specification and recruitment process in place you can think about how to attract the right candidate. If the whole process feels rather overwhelming you could use a recruitment agency or the job centre to pre-screen and shortlist suitable candidates for you. They will need to be fully briefed on your selection criteria and need feedback on the candidates they put forward but this can save you a great deal of time. You will have to pay a recruitment agency a fee for their help so shop around and make sure you select one that has experience in your field. You could consider asking your coach or mentor to be part of your selection panel so that you have someone else making observations and perhaps seeing the things you miss. At least it will give you someone to talk your decision through with.

If you're going to do the recruitment yourself you will need to think how you will advertise the vacancy to produce the best possible pool of candidates to choose from. Think about how you will 'sell' the opportunity and encourage people to apply, this is another marketing task so revisit the last chapter. Local papers are not as prevalent or as well read as they used to be so advertising your vacancy there may not be cost effective unless the fee also includes some online promotion. Consider advertising on local jobs boards and social media, especially LinkedIn. Take care when advertising online though because you might be deluged with applications, think how you will deal with them. Is there someone who could help you with pre-screening for instance?

Pre-employment checks

You will need to take up references for your chosen candidate. Ideally you want to hear from former employers but education or character references can be helpful too. You are also obliged to check that the person is who they say they are and has the right to work in the UK. Search 'right to work in UK' on www.gov.uk for the latest information on what is required. You may also have to carry out special checks if your new employee will be working with children or vulnerable adults.

Being a responsible employer

Once you have agreed terms with your new employee you will need to supply these in writing. You should also have a staff handbook that explains things like holidays, sickness entitlements, policies etc. There's a lot of guidance at www.acas.org. You'll need to make sure that you comply with wage and working hours legislation too.

It's worth remembering that most people are only motivated by money when they don't feel fairly recompensed so whilst a competitive wage is important, things like personal development, recognition and support often count more highly. Whilst your budget might restrict how much you can pay your new employee, spending time developing them and making them feel valued should help grow their loyalty and ensure that they are giving the desired impression of your brand. If your business is a limited company you could consider an employee share scheme as a form of reward. This can be a useful way to reward employees when cash is tight and gives them an incentive to help you to grow the company.

As your employee is likely to be fully involved in many aspects of the business they may well hear feedback and generate ideas that you should listen to. Your challenge is to find the right balance between involving your employee and maintaining your authority in case it is needed.

Onboarding

Take time to plan your employee's induction into your business. Order any equipment that they will need to be able to do their job and any items of uniform you want them to wear. Think whether you would like them to have a name badge.

It's a good idea to develop an induction checklist to ensure that you cover the key information they need. Different people learn in different ways. Some like to be thrown in at the deep end, some like to watch a demonstration before having a go themselves, some like to have everything explained with the reasons for doing things a certain way, and some like an opportunity to practise in a safe environment before being exposed to a real-life situation. Try to find out your new employee's preferred learning style and use that to design a personalised induction programme.

It's very easy to overload a new employee on day one which can be so off-putting that some don't return for day two! Try to find a balance between training and giving the employee something meaningful, but not too stressful, to do. Make it easy for your new person to ask questions when they haven't understood or when they haven't remembered all the instructions. A manual that they can refer to can be really helpful. Build in lots of early opportunities to practise. If things have to be done in a particular way make sure that your new employee understands why.

Think how you will check that learning has taken place and that your new staff member is confident to work without supervision. Make it clear what decisions they have the authority to make and when and how they should refer to you.

Managing performance

Most of us like to get feedback on our performance, to know what we do well and to identify those areas where we need to improve. Whether or not you decide to have a formal appraisal process you should think about how you will review your employee's performance periodically. You should also think about how you will make it easy for your staff to share ideas and raise concerns with you. Perhaps an informal chat every couple of months would work for your business. By instigating a process you should avoid the problem of only ever discussing performance when you have a criticism to make! Remember to thank your staff regularly and to praise them for a job well done. Criticisms should always be done in private but recognition can be more valuable when delivered in public.

Dealing with problems

It's a good idea to take advice from an employment lawyer or HR consultant before you start disciplinary or dismissal procedures as we discussed in chapter 5. Many employers have lost tribunal cases because the process was deemed unfair to the employee rather than the decision itself being wrong. This doesn't mean that you shouldn't nip problems in the bud. One of the defences employees have used successfully is that of custom and habit... they haven't been told promptly that their behaviour or practice was unacceptable and have, not unreasonably, assumed that all was well. An informal conversation explaining what you are unhappy about and what changes you would like to see should sort most problems out. The key is in monitoring future performance to ensure that the employee has changed their behaviour.

Interns and work experience

You may find that a local college or university would welcome work placements or internships for their students. These can be a great way to bring in some higher-level skills and get a project done for relatively little cost; there may even be some funding available to support the programme.

You should think carefully about the advantages and disadvantages before committing to such an arrangement. On the one hand, a good student will inject fresh ideas and perhaps develop an aspect of the business that you've been struggling to find time for. On the other hand, the planning and support required may take more time than you can spare.

You should also think about how you will recompense your student. As the mother of a fairly recent intern I'm very much in the camp that says long-term interns should be paid and that every form of work experience should be constructed to give the student a valuable experience. It's worth looking at covering your student's expenses at the very least as the way you treat them can affect your business' reputation.

Finding a sounding board

Running a business can be lonely. Who do you go to for advice? Where can you go to bounce ideas around? How will you celebrate your wins? Many business owners go to their families but unless your family members are in business the advice you get may not be what you need to hear.

A coach can help you structure your thinking and sort your priorities but you should expect to pay for this service. I have found having a coach extremely valuable when I was really clear what I wanted to get out of the relationship. A good coach will help you to explore your options, offer ideas you may not have thought of, challenge your thinking to ensure you have considered all the angles and support you to achieve your goals. Chemistry is important when working with a coach, you need someone whom you can respect and whose personal style is right for you. Most coaches will offer a no-cost or low-cost short consultation for you to check out the chemistry between you. Before you book the session, check out the coach's website and/or social media pages, maybe they have some YouTube videos, review their packages and terms of business so that you only do a trial session with someone whose packages are within your budget and right for your needs. It's a waste of your time and the coach's if you have no intention of following through and can affect your reputation.

An alternative is mentoring, which allows you to access advice from experienced business people. Some mentors offer their services on a voluntary basis. You may find schemes available locally through your council or chamber of commerce or you could visit http://www.mentorsme.co.uk. A mentor will usually provide you with a sounding board, offer suggestions based on their experience and help you to reach decisions. A mentor will not do your job for you but neither will a coach.

Many business-networking organisations encourage their members to support each other and run training and business development events. Perhaps you could be paired with another member to act as each other's accountability partner. My own favourite networking organisation, Fabulous Women and Marvellous Men, offers a mastermind group as part of its highest level membership, The Inspirer Club.

Another option is to join a supportive group of fellow business owners on Facebook or LinkedIn. I'd love you to join me at https://www.facebook.com/groups/Foundedafter40/ where you can connect with other readers and post your questions and ideas. I find my membership of the Female Entrepreneur Association very valuable with online support from fellow members and occasional events in the real world, www.femaleentrepreneurassociation.com. The FEA offers members the chance, once a month, to pair up with a fellow member as an accountability partner. Could you find a similar option?

In summary...

- Trying to do everything yourself can be a false economy. There are many ways of getting the help you need
- Outsourcing tasks can be a flexible option. Suitable providers can be found in your network or by using a number of online brokerage sites
- Take a professional approach to recruiting staff seeking advice where needed and plan training and induction carefully to make sure that your new employee feels welcome and can become effective quickly
- Monitor performance on an ongoing basis and deal with concerns promptly
- Check out your legal obligations before recruiting or terminating an employee
- Your local higher education institution may be able to provide you with an intern or work experience student to help with a specific project

- Finding someone with whom you can talk through ideas and challenges can be invaluable and there are a range of free or paid ways to do this

To get you thinking...

- How will your business operate when you are on holiday, indisposed or overloaded with work?
- Who will help you work through your ideas and challenges to enable you and your business to thrive?

Action points...

- Think through all the tasks that need to happen in your business and decide how they will get done
- If you are planning to recruit staff produce the documentation you need including a staff handbook and recruitment documents

Chapter **13**

Managing the business

'**Everything should be made as simple as possible, but not simpler.**'

—Albert Einstein

You've probably realised by now that there's a lot involved in running a business. It's very easy to spend all your time meeting the needs of your customers but if you don't devote some of your time to managing the business you could get some nasty surprises. That's why a formal business plan includes a section on managing the business and it's why you should give that some thought even if you don't intend to complete a formal plan.

If your past experience is in a corporate environment where there was a department for everything it can come as a bit of a shock to realise that you are now everything from MD to tea maker! There is no PA ordering the stationery (unless you've appointed one) and nobody bringing in the customers unless you have your marketing under control. There is nobody monitoring the finances or measuring marketing effectiveness unless you make it happen. Your plan therefore needs to identify how you will manage the different functions and activities that will make your business successful. The following headings should help structure your thinking:

- Customer service delivery: if you completed the customer journey map in chapter 10 you should have a plan
- Sales and marketing: much of this will also be on your customer journey map but you may need to think about developing new material and keeping your website and social media current
- Administration: list all the activities that need doing, their frequency and any deadlines
- Purchasing: think about raw materials, packaging, stationery, equipment and coffee!
- Financial control: include invoicing, paying bills, paying in money, bank reconciliation, cost and credit control, cash flow management, forecasting, analysis
- Research and development: this might include developing new products or services, customer satisfaction measurement, competitor analysis and new opportunities
- Logistics including premises, vehicle and equipment maintenance
- Information technology: think anti-virus, data protection, backup systems, software updates, computer crashes, mobile phones and tablets
- Statutory obligations: how will you stay up to date with the law as it affects your business? Revisit chapter 5 to see which areas of the law you most need to think about. Also think about tax, company returns etc.
- Staffing: how will you manage and inspire your staff, how will you review performance? See chapter 12 for more information

You will also want to think about how you manage key dates and ad hoc activities etc. Things like:

- Insurance renewals
- Software renewals
- Tax returns
- Membership renewals
- Contract renewals
- Vehicle and equipment servicing
- Domain name and webhosting renewals
- Companies House returns
- Car tax
- Licences

You may find it helpful to set up reminders on your computer or phone but what happens if your hard disk crashes or your phone is stolen? We've been there! These days, cloud computing allows us to back up information so that we can access it from anywhere – no longer do we have to spend hours transferring files when we buy another computer. Even more importantly, when we have a system disaster we still have our files but that only works when we do the backup regularly so build that into your routines. Whatever system you choose, ensure that your key files are backed up at an offsite location. In the event of a fire or other major catastrophe your offsite backup could be your business' saviour.

There are those of us who still favour pen and paper so keeping a list of key dates and plotting them into each new diary can help. I like to record the due date and a reminder that it's coming a couple of weeks before.

Passwords

Wasn't life easier before we had to have a password for everything? However, we can't turn back the clock and passwords are vital to our security so find a system that works for you and a way to remember what password goes where. These days you can get software or apps to manage your passwords or get clever with an

Excel spreadsheet but make sure that you protect your passwords and change them frequently. If you need to share a password and login details with a member of staff or a contractor change them when the person leaves or the contract is ended. You don't want someone with a grudge to have access to your systems; you might find yourself locked out of your own business!

Organisation

You don't want to be wasting time looking for things so establish sound filing and organisation systems from the start. There's been talk of the paperless office ever since computers became mainstream but, if anything, we now have more paper not less. It's vital to keep this under control with systematic filing systems that work for you and anyone else who works in your business. Think too about how you will maintain the filing system so that you don't keep things for longer than you need them. I have found a strange phenomenon at work: whenever I do a major office de-clutter I win some new business! There's no rhyme or reason for this and it's certainly not a recommended marketing technique but it seems to happen every time I have a good clear out. It's like I have created space for someone new to enter, perhaps it could work for you too.

Remember that there are some files that you will need to retain or display for statutory purposes, for example tax records, health and safety information, and insurance certificates. Typically, self-employed people will need to retain tax records for five years from the deadline for filing those records, usually 31st January. So if you file your 2016/2017 return on or before 31st January 2018 you will need to keep the records until 31st January 2023. If you have premises you may need to display a health and safety poster or first aid box information etc.

If you take on an apprentice or employ someone on a contract of service you will need to display an up to date employers' liability insurance certificate, failure to do so can result in a fine of up to £2,500 per day and if you can't show the certificate to a Health and Safety Executive Inspector when asked there is a fine of £1000.

Data protection

There are strict rules for the management of personal data. If you hold information about other people you may need to register with the Information Commissioner's Office, find out by visiting www.ico.org.uk. Whether you have to register or not you will need systems that keep people's information safe and up to date and you must ensure that you don't collect and save more information than you need and that you don't keep it for longer than is reasonable. The law also governs who you can share information with.

A word of warning: there are a number of 'so-called' businesses that will offer to do your data protection registration for you for a fee; avoid them! Registering with the Information Commissioner's Office is easy and inexpensive; you can find the current fee on the website.

Your business environment

When you start a business there's the temptation to want to set up your workspace perfectly from the off, you convince yourself that you need a new desk, filing cabinet, computer etc. However, this can lead to you spending precious cash on things that will not improve your business' performance. Before you spend any money ask yourself, 'How will this expenditure increase my sales or profit?' As a general rule of thumb only spend on those items that will contribute directly to sales, or save you time or money. Unless the item you want to buy will affect the customer's experience, second hand will be fine. So if you meet clients in your office you will need to make sure that the furniture creates the right impression and is suitable for your brand. However, if your office is off limits to your clients you can make do with mismatched furniture so long as it is safe and serves the purpose you need.

 If you do have customers coming to your premises then it's really important that you manage that space. The morning inspection was a discipline drilled into me in my early days at Marks & Spencer and it is well worth following. When you start your day put on your customer-vision spectacles. Look at what your customer will see and make sure that you are creating the right impression. Look out for things like trip hazards, peeling paint or ripped carpets, out of date notices, locks that are missing (e.g. in the toilet), dust and dirt, displays that are tired or untidy etc. It can be a good idea to develop a checklist that you go through on a regular basis to make sure that you don't miss anything. We do tend to stop seeing things we encounter all the time.

Managing business performance

Most of the business owners I speak to admit that they don't track or measure as much data as they should in their businesses. However, it's worth remembering that what gets measured can be improved. Again, going back to my days in Marks & Spencer we had lots of targets but amongst those tracked on a daily basis were sales and staffing. We had a target that was referred to as takings per head, arrived at by dividing the takings by the full-time equivalent of staff used to take them. Every afternoon the takings for the day would be counted and we would measure actual performance against target; that meant that we could adjust staffing for the remainder of the week to ensure that we came in on target in the final analysis. I'm not suggesting that you necessarily need to track your performance daily but you should be measuring on a monthly or activity basis.

So what should you track? Here are some ideas:

- Sales
- Costs
- Ratio of costs to sales
- Average spend per customer
- Average time taken for clients to pay invoices
- Time taken to turn enquiries into orders
- Time to fulfil orders

It's also really important to measure the effectiveness of your marketing activities so some of the things you should be looking at include:

- Open rates for emails and the times of day, days of the week, headlines etc. that get the best response
- Click-through rates for emails (how many people click on hyperlinks in your emails)
- Enquiries generated
- Sales made
- Cost per lead, per sale etc.
- Average lifetime value of a customer
- Social media performance
- Website hits, enquiries and sales etc.

You should measure the effectiveness of individual activities and campaigns as well as your routine marketing. For example, you should be tracking open rates, click throughs and sales from your regular newsletters so that you can make changes where necessary. You will want to know if your investment in advertising at a particular location or in a specific publication is working. If you have an integrated marketing campaign, say Facebook advertising, email newsletters, a PR campaign and local advertising, you want to know which parts work best. Make it as easy as possible for people to tell you, for example if you are advertising in a variety of publications include a different enquiry code in each one or use different email addresses or even telephone numbers for each media. There are companies that can offer tracking services for you.

When you are measuring performance compare your actual numbers against your forecasts and against suitable comparative figures. So you might compare one month with the next as well as year on year. Be careful when measuring against historical numbers because there can be factors that can skew the comparisons. For example, Easter moves every year so if your sales are influenced by the holiday period you will need to compare the figures for Easter one year against the previous Easter. The weather and local and national events can also boost or decimate your numbers on particular dates and I guarantee that you will struggle to recall the reasons when you look back a year later, so make sure that you record the reasons for unusual fluctuations. For example, a local pub might find takings boosted when a big football match is on the big screen whereas their restaurant neighbours may find their takings hit because everyone is next door!

As your business becomes established, having access to your historical data will help you to establish any patterns that can help you with the planning. For example, a local restaurant client of mine knows that the Wimbledon tennis fortnight is not good for business! Knowing this kind of information can help you to work out when taking a holiday will have minimum impact on your business or when you might need to bring in extra help. It will also help you to work out when to programme your marketing activities and if you are measuring the results of your marketing you will be really clear about the lead time between activity and impact so will know exactly how to schedule your campaigns.

> ## Some monitoring tips and examples from our business owners...
>
> - **Monica Castenetto** of Live a Life You Love keeps spreadsheets to monitor hits on her website and visits to her blog. She makes a point of checking interest in her blog when she has promoted it on social media. She also monitors progress through her sales funnel
> - **Giles Button** is an advocate of checklists believing that they are a great aid to systematising your business which is a key to growth
> - **Roy Summers** of Bodyline Fitness is a great believer in tracking numbers. Roy sets targets for number of visits to the gym, new clients, trainer hours etc. and measures them all at least once a month. Although his is a very local business his website is one of his most effective marketing tools so he updates it three to four times a week and regularly monitors its performance. As a result Roy's business has been growing consistently for the last five years

Getting over your excuses!

Some of us are naturally good at numbers whereas some of us convince ourselves that we can't do them, probably because of years studying maths and struggling with algebra or logarithms! If numbers are not your thing then find ways to get the data produced for you. That might mean running reports from within your accounting package, using the analytics programmes for your online activities e.g. Google, Facebook and your email marketing host. Alternatively, pay someone to set up the systems to collect key data automatically for you and feed it into an Excel spreadsheet or similar programme. Ask your accountant to produce monthly or quarterly performance reviews and the same with your marketing consultant.

The important thing is not how you get to your numbers but what you do with them. Whilst you can outsource their production and ask for advice in interpreting them it's important that you really interrogate them yourself and understand what they are telling you. Try to find a way to benchmark your numbers against typical numbers for your type of business or particular activities. Your accountant or marketing adviser may be able to give you some comparative numbers or you may be able to source them through your trade association or even an internet search.

Specialist advice

What are the areas of your business that make you feel vulnerable? Perhaps you need legal agreements for every contract or maybe you need specialist health and safety advice. You should identify those areas where you feel you need support and work out how you will get that help. You could sign up to a scheme that gives you easy access to a lawyer; several small business membership bodies offer such deals as part of their member benefits. Alternatively, you might agree to pay a retainer fee to a specialist, for example an HR consultant, in order to have support when you need it.

Getting specialist support...

*Financial adviser **Alastair Lyon** buys into back office support as part of his industry compliance package. This ensures that he has a system that allows him to deliver a quality service whilst also meeting industry standards.*

Thinking through these things at the planning stage of your business will reduce your stress levels if you have a crisis and, if you are seeking funding for your business, will be more likely to impress potential backers.

In summary...

- You may be running a small business but all the functions of business still need to be covered, if not by you then who?
- You will need systems and reminders to make sure that you don't miss key dates or activities
- Your paperwork and computer files will need organising so that you can easily find things when you need them
- Control your passwords and change them when staff or contractors who had access move on
- You must decide whether or not you need to be registered with the Information Commissioner's Office
- Spending on your working environment should be limited to what is seen by your customers and maintains your brand's position
- Numbers are vital to managing your business' performance, decide which ones are important to you and find ways to collate and monitor them
- We all need specialist advice from time to time, planning where you will source this can save stress in a crisis

To get you thinking...

- What are all the different functions and activities that need to happen for my business to thrive and who will do them?
- What are the key dates and documents I need to plan in my diary?
- What equipment and furniture is vital for my business to start?
- How will I know how my business is performing and where I need to make changes?
- Which aspects of running my business make me feel vulnerable and who can support me?

Action points...

- Decide how you will manage the key functions in your business and identify any specialists you will use
- Agree terms with your chosen specialists
- Set up tracking systems for monitoring your business' performance and block out time in your diary once a month to use them

Chapter **14**

Launching the business

'The way to get started is to quit talking and start doing.'
—Walt Disney

By now you should be ready to start your business. This is where I see so many people hesitate. They think they need to do a bit more research, do another training course or wait until one more jigsaw piece slots into place. Rarely is the hesitation justified. It's an excuse brought about by fear. They are frightened of failure but you can't succeed in what you don't start.

Let me tell you that you will never feel 100% prepared. There will always be something else to learn but the best way to learn is from experience. You can buy in the skills you don't have yet. You can adapt your plans in the light of experience.

If you have worked your way through this book you should now have a plan in place. You should have:

- Defined your ideal customer
- Identified the problem they have that you can solve
- Understood their decision-making process

- Found your competitive advantage
- Decided on your route to market
- Set your prices
- Raised any finance you need
- Designed your systems and processes
- Developed your marketing plan
- Worked out how you will get any help you need

 So you are ready to start. No excuses. Your time has arrived. So what will you need to do before you can launch? I'm talking about absolute essentials here, not the nice to do, not another excuse to prevaricate! I'm talking about things like signing the lease on premises, buying or making stock, ordering packaging, setting up your bank or PayPal account, making your website live etc. How long will it take you to complete these activities? When you have worked this out you can set your start date. Set a date that is realistic but motivating. Share it publicly and ask your mentor or support team to make you accountable.

How will you launch?

Some business owners like to launch with a big fanfare that creates lots of buzz and brings plenty of footfall to the opening. But this has its risks. We've all heard about the traffic jams created by the opening of a new branch of IKEA and the long waits for service when a new restaurant can't cope with demand. For these reasons you might be better to go for a soft launch.

It's worth remembering that you never have a second chance to create a good first impression. A soft launch allows you to test your product or service with a limited audience before you go for the big time. This means that you have time to test your systems, train your support team and tweak your offer before launching to a wider public. It means that you can iron out any difficulties before they cause you a major problem. Of course it also means that it will take longer for the business to start making money so you will need to factor this in to your financial projections.

Should you 'do a launch'? ...

Many of the business owners featured in this book simply started trading; they didn't do a launch event of any kind. Whilst there's nothing wrong with this, most report that it took a significant amount of time to start growing the business.

*On the other hand, **Gilles and Claire Pelenc** have done a number of launches for both of their businesses. When they launched their Forever network marketing business they invited a select group of people to their home for product and business opportunity presentations: two events netted them 20 customers and five new team members.*

Each time they have started a new Athena women's network group they have done a big launch event using their networking connections and social media to pull together a guest list. Their most successful launch had 70 people attending of whom 25 joined.

The soft launch

 If you are going for the soft launch think what you want it to achieve. Do you want to test your offer or get testimonials to use in your marketing? Which systems or processes do you want it to test? What kind of sales will test them? How many customers do you need for the test to give you the answers you seek? What kind of customers do they need to be and how will you find them? This is where your friends and family might be able to help before you go out to your target market. But don't rely just on your friends and family, you need to get some engagement and feedback from your target market. The best test and the most useful testimonials will come from genuine customers who have no existing relationship with you.

Ideally you will have been building a marketing list, or at least some social media connections, as you've been developing your business plan so these are the people to invite to your soft launch. If your list is tiny then you can invite everyone but if it's larger you may wish to stagger the invitations in case they all take you up on it at once. If you need more people ask these connections to bring others with them or promote to local groups that represent your target market.

Do you need to offer your early customers some form of inducement to encourage them to try you out? You may decide to offer a limited number of customers a deal on their first purchase if bought by a specific date. This will reduce the customer's risk and give you the potential to develop your service, gather case studies or collect testimonials. But do keep the offer tight to a limited number of people and/or a tight deadline. You don't want to find yourself offering cut-price deals for months.

Deciding upon your guest list

Who do you want to invite to your launch? Drawing up a potential guest list should be one of your first actions in planning your launch event. This will determine the type of event and the size of the venue you need. If you are working with a PR company they should be able to help especially with media contacts. Think about:

- Journalists, influential bloggers and media representatives
- Sponsors and backers
- Local business organisations
- Local 'celebrities' and influencers
- Your ideal customers
- Your network
- Friends and family

- Staff, advisers and supporters and their friends and family

Are you going to make the event invitation only or do you plan to make it an open invitation or somewhere in between i.e. you invite a set number of guests and their plus ones?

Going for the big razzmatazz

You might decide to launch with a big bang in order to attract maximum publicity to put your business on the map. Whether you do this from day one or following a soft launch period will depend upon the nature of your business and how confident you are that everything will work properly from the outset.

Decide what you want to achieve with your launch. Is it to get prospects across the threshold or is your main priority to generate media coverage? Your launch event will need to be designed to meet your objective. Whilst inviting a celebrity to cut the ribbon at a party might work, unless you can attract a name that is highly popular with your target market or such a big name as to attract local buzz, it may not generate as much interest as you hope. The media like good stories and prefer something unusual or less predictable. Your launch is time to get creative. As we've already seen Richard Branson is known for his creative launches which often involve dressing up. He's dressed as a bride to publicise his Virgin Brides brand, a Zulu warrior to promote flights to South Africa and Elvis to launch a route to Las Vegas. What would work for you? Would combining your launch with support for a local charity night get attention?

It's important that whatever you do is consistent with your brand and will attract your target audience. You will also need to think about location and budget. If your aim is to get people across your threshold you will need to design your event around the size of your premises. If you can't accommodate large numbers at a time you might want to host some form of drop in event lasting several hours. This can be tricky to manage as you might be bursting at the seams one minute but empty when the journalist you want to impress arrives! Think how you can manage that, for instance would timed tickets work or do you need to have friends and family members on hand to fill the gaps?

If you are not using your own premises then can you find a location that is a little unusual or not generally open to the public to host your event? The opportunity to go to an exclusive venue can be another incentive to encourage people to attend. Think about the nature of your business and the type of venue that may connect with it. For example, if you are in the travel industry then a tourist destination might be a good location or could you partner with a service provider, perhaps a vintage bus company? If you are an interior designer would one of your suppliers have space to host your event whilst also showcasing a process that would be interesting to your guests, for example fabric production or wallpaper printing?

Bring in the professionals

If you are going for the big event then do consider bringing in professional help to organise it. An event management company or party planner may have ideas you haven't thought of, will have contacts that could be useful and will think of all the little details that will make your event a success. Try to find someone who has experience of organising business or product launches and who will know what works and what doesn't. If you are working with a PR company they may have existing relationships with event planners which you can take advantage of.

 Make sure that whoever you hire really understands your brand and what you are trying to achieve. Create a proper brief for the event and agree the terms of your contract in writing so you know exactly what you are paying for and who is responsible for what. Set a realistic budget for the type of event you want to host and work out how that budget is allocated. You'll want money for the venue, for the catering and for marketing and publicity as well as paying for the professional help and any entertainment or giveaways that you have planned.

If funding is an issue consider whether you could get another business to sponsor an aspect of the event. For instance, a local off-licence may sponsor the drinks, a local retailer may sponsor the food and an entertainer may be willing to appear in return for publicity. Ideally you want to look for partner companies that share your target audience but in a non-competitive way. Remember to sell what's in it for them when you approach another business to ask for support.

If sponsorship isn't an option and your budget is too tight to pay for professional help to plan the event do at least try to find money for help at the event itself. You want to be free to host the event, to talk to your guests and to promote your business. If you are running around blowing up balloons, filling glasses and preparing food you will be distracted from your purpose. Using a caterer to provide and serve food and drinks will relieve the pressure. If you really can't find the money to pay for professional help do you have friends or family who you could rely on to do a professional job? If not then forget the big launch until you can afford to fund it properly.

Invitations and publicity

Once you have a date for your event you want to get it in the diary of those people who are critical to its success. If you are booking a celebrity or entertainment you may well have checked the date with them before booking the venue but if you want to get local dignitaries or local media people along it could be worth a phone call or an email to get your intended guests to save the date prior to formal invitations going out.

If you are doing an invitation-only event you may wish to send a printed invitation with an RSVP by a deadline to help you to plan catering. Alternatively you may wish to send email invitations via an online booking platform. This will allow people to book at the click of a button and give you instant access to a list of guests so you can send last minute reminders and print off a list of guests for your reception team.

If you are planning an open event you will need to think about how you will publicise it. Will you use social media, local advertising, networking, a leaflet drop or something else? Do you want people to book (a good idea if you are offering catering) or can people just drop in? If you want them to book how will you manage the bookings? Again an online booking tool will help and may be free if you are not charging for admission.

Whilst your launch event is promotion for your business there can be some advantages to charging for attendance. Selling tickets will give you definite numbers for planning, and ticket purchasers are much more likely to be committed to attending your event. However, if you are going to charge you either need to make sure that there is a benefit to the guests, such as networking with other business owners, or that buying a ticket contributes to a charity or good cause.

Make it memorable

You want your launch to get people talking about your new business long after the event and in a good way so you want to make it memorable. Should you have some form of entertainment, for example music or a magician or dance troop? Should you arrange demonstrations or opportunities to try out your products or services? Would a tour of your venue be interesting to your attendees?

Think about hiring a photographer or videographer to capture the event. Invite your guests to take photos and videos to share on social media, give them the hashtag you would like them to use to create a buzz about the event. If you have a celebrity in attendance and he or she is willing then perhaps you could give your guests the chance of a photo (even a selfie) with your star guest or even the opportunity to talk.

 Of course things don't always go according to plan so think how you will deal with potential problems. I remember going to a launch event for an art exhibition some time ago. We found ourselves queuing outside for at least half an hour on a bitterly cold night then had to go and find our own drinks when we finally got in and within half an hour the lights failed and guests were left trying to look at the art via the flashlights on their mobile phones! When it became clear that the power failure wasn't going to be fixed in the short term the organisers terminated the event early. Sadly I remember this event for all the wrong reasons but there were things that the organisers could have done to mitigate the disaster. They could have managed the queue better, they could have organised waiters to give people a drink on arrival and when they sent us home they could have given us a ticket to return free of charge during the exhibition. If they couldn't have managed that on the evening they could have emailed us all the following morning with an apology and an invitation to revisit free of charge and they could have done more to promote the artists who were paying to exhibit at the event. You don't want your guests to have a similar experience so just think what could go wrong and how you could handle it.

If you are planning a party with lashings of alcohol think about offering your guests transport home, perhaps you could do a deal with a local taxi firm. If your target market is mums of young children perhaps you could organise a crèche or include details of childminding services in your invitation. It's these little details that can make a difference.

Think also about your party bags! Everyone loves a freebie so think what would be valuable to your guests. Try to be original and relevant with your giveaways. A branded pen and notepad may be relevant to a training company but some sample cosmetics would be more appropriate for a spa business. A food business might give away tasters. Roy Summers of Bodyline Fitness gave away branded water bottles, highly relevant for personal training clients. I have given away a mini marketing action guide to an audience of small business owners.

How will you promote your business at the event?

The main reason for hosting a launch event is to promote your business so it's really important to devote plenty of time to thinking how you will do this. This is not the time for flying by the seat of your pants!

Are you going to do a demonstration, a tour, a presentation or just a short talk? Are you going to give away samples? Will you show people your website or give them copies of your marketing materials? All of these things require planning and time for execution. If you are launching your business and website at the same time do your web developers know when the launch date is and can they deliver on time? Have you allowed sufficient time for copywriting, design and printing of your marketing materials? How long do you need to write and practise your presentation or talk? Don't be tempted to cut corners because this is your one opportunity to make a great first impression.

How much of your personal journey will be of interest to your audience? Don't be tempted to overindulge in your own story. I remember one conference where a speaker started by saying too many people got caught up in their personal stories and then proceeded to spend the next 20 minutes telling hers! She was right; she lost her audience after about five minutes because she spent too long on a subject that was all self-promotion. Striking the balance isn't easy but if you keep asking yourself why your audience should be interested then you will probably get close.

Think what you want your audience to do at the end of your presentation and work back from there. Do you want them to book an appointment, give your marketing materials to their associates or visit your website? Give your listeners a reason to take the action you want them to take and perhaps incentivise them to take the action whilst it's still fresh in their mind. Perhaps a limited time offer or a reward for introducing a friend. You do want attendees to understand what your business is and how they could benefit from your service and also how they could help you to become a success.

 Many business owners choose to thank their supporters during their launch event. If you are going to do this make a list, the last thing you want to do is to upset someone because you left them out! Again it's a question of finding a balance, if you have a really long list it might be better to list people in a newsletter or as a handout rather than naming them all in your talk. However, if you have sponsors helping you to cover the cost of your event or backers who have helped you to get the business off the ground you should mention them.

Dealing with the media

The chances are that you will invite members of the media to your launch in the hope that they will cover your event. You should make it as easy as possible for them to do so. Prepare a press pack to give them the key information that they need, include some product samples or an invitation to try out a service at your expense. Give them some photographs and some quotes that they can use if there isn't time for an interview, better still schedule time for an interview before or after your launch.

Try to make time to speak to media representatives during the event. This is where it helps to have a PR consultant on hand to make sure you are introduced but if this isn't possible brief whoever is on reception to tell you when members of the press arrive and to point out who's who.

After the event send out a short press release with some quality photographs which showcase your business and the event. Do check the photos carefully to make sure they create the right impression, you don't want a picture with someone looking bored or one that suggests no one was present!

Maximising your return on investment

Your launch should have generated a buzz amongst the people who attended but you want the ripples to spread further so make sure that you and your guests are active on social media sharing photos and comments about the event and your business. Monitor what people are saying and deal constructively with any criticisms. Don't get defensive. Thank people for bringing the matter to your attention and say how you will deal with it. Share all the positive comments widely and use them in your marketing, ideally with the permission of the person giving the testimonial so that you can use their full name.

Follow up with the people who attended. Ask them for feedback, invite them to come again or ask them to recommend you. Remind them about any special promotions and tell them what was in their goody bag; they may not have looked!

Try to keep the momentum going by being active on social media and show up at local events. Thank journalists for featuring your story and build on those relationships as much as you can. If a journalist knows that you will help them with a quote or an introduction when they are on a tight deadline they are likely to feature your stories when the opportunity is right. It's worth recognising that most print media is now produced on a shoestring with fewer and fewer journalists working on wider remits and tighter deadlines. If you can help them to fill their pages with stories that will interest their reader and which aren't blatant advertising you have a good chance of being featured especially if you have a relationship with the journalist or editor. Remember to share their stories on your social media and not just the ones that feature you!

In summary...

- You'll never be 100% ready to start so set a start date and stick to it
- A soft launch will allow you to test your systems and processes in a controlled manner before you go for a big take up
- Think about the type of people you want to invite to your launch before you decide on the type of event, venue etc.
- Decide on your objectives for your launch so that you can plan the type of event that will meet them
- Set a budget and think about hiring professional help to share the strain
- Decide how you will invite people or publicise your event and get in the diaries of key people as soon as possible
- Work out how to make the event memorable and source any giveaways you want to include
- Prepare a press pack and invite key media people
- Follow up after the event

To get you thinking...

- How much time do you need before you can open your doors for business?
- Do you need to test systems and processes before dealing with high volume customers?
- How can you make your event different, memorable and attractive to your target audience and the media?
- What type of event would be consistent with your brand?
- Who do you know that would be a draw to get people to your launch or who could introduce you to a key person of influence?

Action points...

- Set your launch date and make a public commitment to it
- Decide whether you will do a soft launch or a big bang
- Set a budget for your launch activities
- Prepare your marketing plan based on the type of launch you are going to do

Chapter **15**

What next?

'There's always a new challenge to keep you motivated.'
—Sean Connery

So your launch is over and you are up and running but you might now be feeling a little deflated. This is normal. You've been working hard developing your business idea, turning your idea into a reality and launching your new venture. Your adrenaline levels have probably been high and you are now feeling a bit of a comedown as you develop a new sense of normality. Whilst these feelings may not be unusual you can't afford to let lethargy take hold. It's time to find ways to keep the momentum going.

Whilst you've got your big business goals they can be overwhelming when you hit a slump. Daily challenges may help. Set yourself some mini goals for each day until you get your mojo back. Those goals might include reading some business or self-development books, watching a video to learn a new skill or listening to a motivational podcast. Perhaps you could write a blog post or two sharing your experience of starting a business or maybe you could comment on someone else's. How about introducing some small marketing initiatives such as updating your LinkedIn profile or posting comments on three Facebook pages that reach your target market? Or pick up the phone and call three friends to ask them to introduce your business to people they might know who would benefit from your offer. The key is to set mini challenges that you will do so they need to benefit you or your business in some way and be small enough not to be overwhelming. As you start to see some achievements, however small, you should find yourself growing more confident to tackle some of those bigger goals.

This may be your first experience of the loneliness of the small business owner. One way to overcome this is to surround yourself with other small business owners, preferably those who are a bit further into the journey than you and those who are enjoying some success. These people will understand your challenges, be able to offer ideas on how to overcome them and generally support you. Belonging to a supportive business network can help as we discussed in chapter 11. There are also a number of business support groups online, particularly on Facebook, but take care what you post because you don't want a prospect who is checking you out online to find your angst!

Dealing with slow growth

If you are disappointed with your rate of progress don't be tempted to throw in the towel. Many of the business owners who contributed to this book reported that their businesses took off more slowly than they'd hoped but perseverance and a few small tweaks helped them progress. This is where the concept of marginal gains, introduced so successfully to British cycling by Sir Dave Brailsford and now picked up with great effect by other Olympic sports, comes into play. The idea isn't to make massive changes but to aim for a 1% improvement in many areas.

 For example, would a change of subject line see a 1% improvement in open rates for your newsletters? Could a different call to action see 1% more clicks on your website? How could you increase enquiries and conversions by 1% each? What would a 1% reduction in your costs do to your profits? What would it mean to your clients if you could improve your results for them by 1%? You get the idea. If you look at every aspect of your business and aim for a 1% improvement then things will begin to move forwards. Take a look at the customer journey that you developed in chapter 10 and see how you could make a 1% improvement in each area identified. This needs to be a continuous process so that your business and your profits are continually growing.

Don't be afraid to ask for help. We've already discussed the benefits of an outside perspective on our businesses but it's important that we remain open to feedback and other people's ideas.

There is another lesson we can take from British cycling and that is the focus on the prize. The team acknowledges that it can't win everything so is very clear that the goal is success in the Tour de France and the Olympics. All the effort goes into ensuring that the athletes are at their peak for those events. We talked in chapter 3 about not being able to sell to everyone – this is the business equivalent of not trying to win every event.

If you have followed the advice in this book you will have identified your niche and the problem you want to solve for the people in that niche. If your business is not growing as quickly as you would like take a look at your marketing activity. Are you promoting your business in the right places to reach that niche? Is it really clear what problem you are solving and are you offering benefits that your ideal client would really want? Are you making your offer as risk free as possible with guarantees or by using testimonials for your early customers?

When business is slow to take off too many people make the mistake of adding lots of different offers to the mix. This leads to confusion. You need to hold your nerve. If you got your market research right, have designed an offer that is what your ideal customer wants and have differentiated your business from your competitors then you should have the foundations for a successful business. If that business has not yet taken off then you need to do more marketing or increase the effectiveness of the marketing that you are doing. Revisit chapter 11 and make sure that you are not making any of the classic mistakes outlined. Are you using all the tricks of the trade suggested? Ask some of your ideal clients for feedback on your materials, what appeals, what puts them off? Be open to feedback and act on it. Try at least one new marketing activity.

Business may not always go according to plan, as one of our contributors says...

'Yes I did get to points where I thought of giving up. When I was overwhelmed with too much going on. When I lost motivation when doing a lot of marketing work for seemingly no return in terms of actual paying clients. When I had doubts about "Will this ever generate enough and regular money for me to live on?"

Some of that still happens!

What keeps me going is reconnecting to the 'why' I'm doing this. Each time I do that, it still feels so right that I feel I have NO OTHER WAY but to get through this, move forward, find solutions, learn from what I've done, try something different, and make it work.'

Building on success

Of course your business may well be on track or even exceeding target. I do hope so. Your challenge now is to build on that success and not to become complacent. What's working? Can you apply the marginal gains concept to that so you get even better results? Do more of what's working.

Make sure that you gather testimonials from your clients. Remember, if you can capture them on video and share those on your social media or website they will be very powerful. Do you have a referral process in place that rewards your existing clients for introducing new ones? Remember to tell people about it and remind them from time to time as they are bound to forget.

Success is like a magnet, people are attracted to successful individuals, and customers are attracted to successful businesses, so celebrate your achievements. Contribute to celebrations posts on Facebook, Tweet your wins, share them on LinkedIn, turn them into a story for your next newsletter. Keep a success diary because I guarantee you will forget the details as your business grows and there may be occasions when you could use the story to benefit your business.

Could your business be an award winner? Look out for opportunities to enter small business awards. In many instances entry is by completion of an entry form so your success stories will enhance your entry. The recognition from doing well in a business contest can be a great boost to the self-confidence but is also a good vehicle for some positive PR for your business. Make sure that you promote your achievements widely and don't forget to contact the local and specialist media.

The Pareto Principle or 80:20 rule...

'The best tip I can give to someone who is about to start a business venture is to understand as early as possible the 20% activities that will be responsible for 80% of the turnover/sales/results/recruits/income... and then concentrate 80%++ of their effort on these 20% activities. Keep your nose down, concentrate on the activities, not the immediate results. You'll be glad you did in 6–12 months.' **Gilles Pelenc**

Tweaking the business plan

It's really important to refer back to your business plan on a regular basis, particularly your cash flow forecasts. This is especially important if your progress is significantly different to your original forecasts whether that is better or worse. As we discussed in chapter 9, rapid growth can be a problem if you don't have the cash flow to support it so identifying a potential problem early is vital. If the business is doing well the chances are that your bank will want to support you. However, as we discussed earlier, backers back people as much as they back businesses so your bank manager will be much more impressed if you ask for help with a forecast cash flow problem rather than when you have already run out of money. Be realistic about how much funding you need and decide how you want that support. Do you want a loan so that you can plan around regular repayments? Or would an overdraft give you greater flexibility albeit at a higher interest rate?

Think too about getting help before you overstretch yourself. You don't want to damage the reputation that you've worked so hard to build by being unable to deliver at the same standard. What plans did you make for support? Do they need some adjustments?

If getting help isn't an option then do be upfront with prospects about how long they will have to wait for your time. Some will be willing because they really want to work with you, others may prefer to make alternative arrangements. Is there someone in your network whom you could recommend?

Having other people in your network that you would be willing to refer prospects to when you are too busy can be a very good idea. Your prospect will view the referral as helpful and may then come back to you the next time they have a need. You may also benefit with cross referrals from your competitor when they are busy, a win-win situation.

Take another look at your marketing plan. If business is slow you may need to do more activities but don't be tempted to stop marketing if you're enjoying early success. Stopping marketing is like turning off a tap, eventually the flow stops. Instead think about changing the emphasis of your marketing, promote your achievements, tell people that you're now taking bookings for some date in the future. People will pick up on your success and realise that if they want to work with you they will need to plan ahead and make a commitment.

Your business plan is a working document. It's highly unlikely that everything will go to plan but at least you will have a sound foundation for your decision making. Amending your business plan as you go will keep you focused on working on your business and its development and not just working in the business.

Good luck

Many dream of owning their own business, far fewer make their dreams a reality. Congratulations on coming so far. You are now largely in control of your own destiny. Remember:

- To stay connected to your *'why'*
- To keep an eye on developments in your marketplace
- To stay in touch with the demands of your ideal customer
- To differentiate your business from the competition
- To market your business regularly
- To keep an eye on the numbers, particularly cash flow and profitability
- To build your support network and not be afraid to ask for help

and above all

- To enjoy your new business

Good luck!

In summary...

- You may experience a comedown after the highs of launching, this is normal but needs to be addressed
- Small achievements can help to rebuild momentum
- Many business owners experience slower progress than planned, don't give up but look for marginal gains to move things forward

- Early success can be a problem if you don't manage it. Keep an eye on cash flow and look for ways to get help if you need it
- Your business plan should be a living document that you refer to often and amend regularly

To get you thinking...

- Reconnect with that vision you had for your business in chapter 1. How far have you progressed towards it? What is your next step?

Action points...

- Plot time in your diary at least once a month for monitoring progress and adjusting the business plan
- Make time to celebrate your success, even small wins

Postscript

I hope this book has given you food for thought and many practical steps to help you start your business. Do realise that businesses come in many different forms and that you may still have some questions relevant to your specific type of business. Please visit the website www.foundedafter40.co.uk for more inspiration and ideas, for up to date website links and details of events you might be interested in. Join our Facebook community, www.facebook.com/groups/Foundedafter40/, to share your challenges and successes with others starting the journey and to ask for the help you need.

Meet the contributors

Thank you so much to the following business owners who have shared their insights into running a business.

Alastair Lyon Independent financial adviser	IFA Direct http://www.ifadirect.co.uk
Buki Obakin Childrenswear retailer	Finoora http://www.finoora.co.uk
Cathie O'Dea Travel consultant	Travel Counsellors www.travelcounsellors.co.uk/cathie.odea
Egidija Bailie Natural skincare maker	EE's Cosmetics http://www.ees-cosmetics.co.uk
Giles Button Arbonne consultant and former IT business owner	Arbonne http://gilesbutton.arbonne.com
Gilles and Claire Pelenc Forever Living consultant and Athena regional director	Natural Networkers http://gilles60.wixsite.com/claireandgilles
Jane Hardy Business networking	Fabulous Women and Marvellous Men http://fabulous-women.co.uk
Jill Bennett Arbonne consultant	Arbonne http://jillbennett.arbonne.com

Leonie Wright Nutritionist	Eat Wright http://www.eatwright.co.uk
Lucy Pitts Copywriter	Strood Copy http://www.stroodcopy.co.uk
Maureen Bailey Curtain and soft- furnishings maker	VA Curtains http://vacurtains.co.uk
Monica Castenetto Life coach	Live a Life You Love http://livealifeyoulove.co.uk
Rosanna Henderson Mosaic artist	Rosanna's Mosaics https://rosannasmosaics.com
Roy Summers Personal trainer and training studio owner	Bodyline Fitness http://bodylinestudios.co.uk
Zoe Angle Stained glass designer, maker and repairer	Angle Glass http://www.angleglass.co.uk